D1068894

SELECTED KENTUCKY LITERATURE

SELECTED KENTUCKY LITERATURE

Edited

by

Joy Pennington

ARCHER EDITIONS PRESS

SELECTED KENTUCKY LITERATURE

First Edition

Design by Wanda Hicks

Library of Congress Cataloging in Publication Data

Selected Kentucky literature.
1. American literature—Kentucky.
2. American literature—20th century.
I. Pennington, Joy, 1939—
PS558.K4S4 810'.8'09769 80-17593
ISBN 0-89097-019-X
ISBN 0-89097-020-3 (pbk.)

"How They Chose the Dead" from *How They Chose the Dead* by Hollis Summers. Copyright 1973. Published by Louisiana State University Press. Reprinted by permission of Hollis Summers.

"Ode to a Purple Aluminum Christmas Tree" by Harriette Simpson Arnow. Copyright 1972. Published in *Pegasus*. Reprinted by permission of Harriette Simpson Arnow.

"The Bringer of Water," "The Mad Farmer Revolution," and "Water" from *Farming: A Hand Book*, copyright © 1970 by Wendell Berry. Reprinted by permission of Harcourt Brace Jovanovich, Inc.

"The Contrariness of the Mad Farmer" Copyright © 1968 by Wendell Berry. Reprinted from his volume *Farming: A Hand Book* by permission of Harcourt Brace Jovanovich, Inc.

"The Birth" (Near Port William) Copyright © 1970 by Wendell Berry. Reprinted from his volume *Farming: A Hand Book* by permission of Harcourt Brace Jovanovich, Inc.

"The Reader," "The Guns of Fort Knox," "Wisdom," and "Trappists, Working" from *Collected Poems of Thomas Merton*. Copyright 1946 by New Directions. Copyright 1949 by Our Lady of Gethsemani Monastery. Copyright © 1957 by The Abbey of Gethsemani. Reprinted by permission of New Directions.

"Chad" and "Teaching Children," by Maureen Morehead were published in *Twigs*, Vol. XIII, Fall 1976. Reprinted by permission of Maureen Morehead.

"the purple lady and birth," by Maureen Morehead was published in the *Louisville Review*, No. 2, Spring 1977. Reprinted by permission of Maureen Morehead.

"Segovia's Fingernail" by Lee Pennington was first published in *The Spirit of '76*, 1976 Defiance College. Reprinted by permission of J. R. LeMaster.

"Dawn's Time" by Lee Pennington was first published in *The Album of International Poets of Achievement*. Copyright 1980. Reprinted by permission of Amal Ghose, editor.

"The System," "New Year," "Red Raspberries," and "Maenad" from *White Barn* by Jane Stuart. Copyright 1976. Published by Whipporwill Press. Reprinted by permission of Jane Stuart.

"Mountain Funeral" from *Kentucky is My Land* by Jesse Stuart. Copyright 1952. Reprinted by permission of the Jesse Stuart Foundation.

"Black April" from *Harvest of Youth* by Jesse Stuart. Copyright 1930. Reprinted by permission of the Jesse Stuart Foundation.

"Hold April" from *Hold April* by Jesse Stuart. Copyright 1962. Published by McGraw-Hill. Reprinted by permission of The Jesse Stuart Foundation.

"Be Kind to Dust" from *The World of Jesse Stuart*, ed. J. R. LeMaster. Copyright 1975. Published by McGraw-Hill. Reprinted by permission of The Jesse Stuart Foundation.

The material on the following page constitutes an extension of the copyright page.

For
the Kentucky writers in general,
one in particular.

CONTENTS

PLAYS

INTRODUCTION

Kentucky's literary tradition began with Gilbert Imlay and Thomas Johnson, Jr. Imlay, with the publication of *The Emigrants, or the History of an Expatriated Family, being a Delineation of English Manners drawn from Real Characters,* in 1793, became the state's first novelist. Johnson, with the publication of a collection of poems, *The Kentucky Miscellany* in 1796, became Kentucky's first poet. Because Imlay lived in the state for only eight years, and Johnson was known as the "Drunken Poet" of Danville, mostly writing doggerel, others had to establish Kentucky in American letters. John M. Harney with *Crystalina, A Fairy Tale*, published in 1816, was the first poet to earn a national reputation, but it was James Lane Allen and John Fox, Jr. near the end of the nineteenth century who really gave Kentucky a substantial place in American literature. James Lane Allen, whose career began in 1885 and extended into the twentieth century, wrote in the genteel tradition with the Bluegrass region as his setting while John Fox, Jr., whose career began in 1894 and also extended into the twentieth century, wrote about the mountaineers of eastern Kentucky. Both were widely read and well respected.

Others followed, adding to Kentucky's literary reputation. Madison Cawein, Theodore O'Hara, James T. Cotton Noe, Joseph Cotter, and David Morton were noted poets while Annie Fellows Johnson, Alice Hegan Rice, Irvin S. Cobb, Isabel McLennan McMeekin, Dorothy Park Clark, and Elizabeth Madox Roberts were noted for their prose. These, and other Kentuckians, have written some of the best short stories, poems, plays, and novels in America.

Many have transcended the region to be recognized nationally and internationally. Rebecca Caudill, Harriette Simpson Arnow, James Still, Hollis Summers, Jesse Stuart, and Allen Tate have received numerous literary awards. A.B. Guthrie, Jr. and Robert Penn Warren have won Pulitzer Prizes; in fact, Robert Penn Warren has won the Pulitzer in two different genres, once in fiction and twice in poetry.

Having had an interest for many years in the historical and contemporary literature of Kentucky, I finally began to compile this anthology concentrating on contemporary authors. My first question was "Who is a Kentucky author"? For my purposes here, I decided to use birth or residence to establish writers as Kentuckians. Compiling the book has involved choices, then alternate choices, and, finally, compromises. In general, I have selected these short stories, poems, and plays for their variety of subjects, themes, characters, and styles.

Kentucky writers, like other authors, write about the complexities of life in the twentieth century where nuclear power, computerization, and dwindling natural resources reshape the world. Human relationships involving psychological and social situations, religion, and environment are among the authors' concerns. Through the use of such subjects as Harriette Simpson Arnow's purple aluminum Christmas trees, Thomas Merton's guns of Fort Knox, Robert Penn Warren's dragons, and Janice Holt Giles' electricity, the authors consider our values. Regardless of subject, each author gives order and understanding to a part of our lives that is sometimes sheer chaos.

Themes, too, are varied. A.B. Guthrie in "Ebbie" is concerned with a boy's growing up and the effects of uncontrolled rage while Benjamin Bradford in "Concentric Circles" considers old age, loneliness, and isolation. Hollis Summers in "Bridge Freezes Before Road Surface" explores the dull monotony of life and the sameness of people; on the other hand, Wendell Berry in "The Mad Farmer Revolution" shows a new man making a new Eden out of a crowded, concrete modern world. Other themes include conformity, change, faith, guilt, ignorance, and fanaticism.

Among the characters are small, strong children, mad farmers, middle-aged married couples, young lovers, fanatic disciples, lonely old women, pretentious preachers, and supercilious snobs.

Styles, too, are as individual as subjects, themes, and characters. The prose in Elizabeth Madox Roberts' story, "The Sacrifice of the Maidens," is very poetic while Hollis Summers' poem, "Manual for the Freeway," reads like a rulebook. Some of the stories, including Robert Penn Warren's "The Patented Gate and the Mean Hamburger" are understated, but others, including Jesse Stuart's "Word and the Flesh" are exaggerated and colloquial. Styles in poetry range from Jim Wayne Miller's parody in "Nature Poem Embodying a Truth" to Lee Pennington's satire in "Segovia's Fingernail." Some poets, such as Allen Tate, choose the restrictive sonnet form; others, such as Maureen Morehead, prefer free verse.

Finally, editing this anthology has clearly pointed out to me that Kentucky has every right to be extremely proud of her literary heritage. The state has produced diverse and important talent, and I am happy to bring together in this book some of that talent.

Joy Pennington
Louisville, Kentucky
February 1980

SHORT STORIES

Janice Holt Giles

WHEN THE 'LECTRIC COME TO THE RIDGE

> "As the Appalachian child grows older he begins to shape and form in the mold of his society."
>
> *40 Acres and No Mule*

The boy held his dog to heel while the butterfly, speared by a shaft of sunlight through the woods that bordered the river, teetered over a trumpet flower. "Hit's goin' to light," he whispered to the dog. "Hit's goin' to light an' then we kin see its wings."

The butterfly hovered uncertainly, warmed by the sun, beating its wings ecstatically in the drenching sweetness that poured from the flower. This flower, or that. It was undecided. This deep, unpierced bell of bloom, or that dark, amber tear of honey. Rapturously it circled and dipped over the vine, tipping a wing at a trumpet and then, unable to bear such sweetness, spiraling dizzily upward. Here, there, it flitted, wavering, fluttering, darting. A quiver threaded the ribs of its wings and they spread and dropped over the bell of the trumpet.

A sigh slipped from the boy's throat and his hand touched the dog warningly. He slid one foot noiselessly forward and bent to look. The sun laid a bright bar across his slight shoulders and touched his straw-thatched head with gold. His face tensed and stilled as he looked, and he whispered, "Hit's blue." His mouth quivered and a tremble of excitement shook him. "Hit's blue, with yaller spots. Oh, hit's the purtiest one we've ever seed! Look, Jupe, hit's got red around the aidges!"

The dog had been still as long as he could. He yawned and settled back on his haunches to scratch at a flea. Frightened, the butterfly bent its wings rigidly and then lifted them into startled flight.

"Now see what you done," the boy scolded. "You done skeered it away. Cain't you never be still when yer 'sposed to? Hit was arestin', an' you skeered it away."

The dog whimpered and slid to its belly, inching toward the boy, thumping its tail and licking pleadingly at the boy's feet. It fawned and begged and held its shamed eyes from the beloved face.

The boy relented. "Well, I reckon you never knowed no better. An' if a flea's bitin', I reckon you gotta scratch. But it looks like they're allus bitin' jist when you'd ort to be still. Lost me that squirrel down in the holler other day. An' you done skeered the fishes plumb outen the Beaver Hole chasin' that rabbit jist now. I'd ort to wup you one, that's what I ort to do. But I'll not today. Next time, though, you jist let them thar fleas ketch you."

The dog went wild with joy, knowing he was forgiven, and leaped and plunged and circled and pawed. His tail beat a fast tattoo in the air and he pranced jubilantly. Then he dashed to a fallen tree and dug madly at a groundhog hole. He barked importantly and eyed the boy anxiously. Just see, he said, just see what I've found. "Humph," the boy snorted, "you needn't to be showin' off thataway. That ole den's so old the groundhog's been dead a year. C'mon now. You done ruint the fishin'. Let's go dig some sang." He hauled in his fishing line and took it off the pole. He cast the green cane aside. "C'mon, boy."

They followed a path through the woodsy bottoms, across a field, and began to climb the ridge. The boy's eyes took in the gum and sassafras, the sumach, the heavy veins of dogwood seedlings. Morning dew hung sparkly and brilliant on every leaf and blade, showering a small rain across the path when the dog brushed against the bushes. The boy stopped at a hickory tree and looked closely at the hulls scattered under it. "They's been a squirrel here," he told the dog. "Yestiddy, likely. Them nuts is still fresh. We'll bring the gun an' git him tomorrer."

The dog's ears stood up and his tail went stiff. "Now now, Jupe," the boy said. "We ain't got the gun this time. Tomorrer we'll come back an' git him." The dog let down and trotted back to the path.

When the path cleared the woods and penciled off through a pasture the boy and the dog angled on down the ridge. "Ain't no use lookin' fer sang hereabouts," the boy said. "Wait'll we git down in the holler."

The north face of the ridge swelled gently, easily, shouldering itself toward the deep ravine that gashed it midway. Suddenly the easy slope sheered off abruptly and plunged downward.

Steep and sharp it fell straight down into the holler, its sides patched with thick rugs of moss under the trees. The boy dug in his heels and slid from one bed of moss to another, sinking his feet deep in the soft mat, letting its plush brake him against the downhill pull. The dog scampered ahead, waiting in the easy places.

The floor of the holler was narrow, boxing in a shallow stream that raced rapidly between its walls. White water foamed around the rocks and chattered noisily. The boy and the dog drank deeply and then followed the stream up the holler, branching off into a deeper ravine on the right. Here the floor widened and was bedded with a heavy leaf mold through which a rank growth of small sprouts and plants pushed themselves.

"Now, this is it," the boy said. "Here's whur the sang grows best. I takened notice o' this place last year."

He cut a slender sapling and sharpened it with his big barlow knife. "Right thar by that down tree"—he pointed the stick—"they'll be a patch." The dog laughed and wagged his tail. "You'll see," said the boy. "Jist you wait an' see." They came up to the log. "See thar! I told you hit'd be thar."

Across the log a bed of ginseng lay dark and green, slender stems spiking upward, pronging at the top to bear the soft ivy green leaves. "All of 'em three-prongs," the boy exulted. "No! That's one of 'em a four-prong. See that thar big un next the log, Jupe? See, hit's got four prongs! Oh, hit's untellin' whenever we've found a four-prong un."

Jupiter sniffed the log and hoisted his leg. "You, Jupe!" the boy yelled and the dog fled ignominiously.

Gently the boy dug the plants from their bed and, breaking off the tops, slid the roots into his overalls pocket. "Hit won't take many like them thar to weigh heavy," he said. "We'll have us three-four ounces 'fore you know it. Bet ole John Barry's eyes bug out when we take 'em in the store. Bet he'll be s'prised we got so much. Bet hit'll bring anyways three-four dollars."

When they had cleaned the bed he and the dog wandered on, up the big holler and down it, up the little un and across, always looking for the dark-veined sang whose roots, when dried, were good medicine for so many ailments, and which brought seventy cents an ounce when sold to the country storekeeper at the Gap.

The boy's pockets filled until they bulged and the dark hollers grew bright with the noon-riding sun. A steamy, airless heat rose from the walled ravine. The dog no longer raced ahead. He lay in the shade waiting, his tongue lolling and his sides heaving. The boy's shirt turned dark with sweat. He squinted up into the sun. "Reckon it's about time to go home," he decided. "Dinner'll be ready time we git thar."

He whistled to the dog and they started the steep climb out. The boy was reaching for a root to pull up by when he stopped abruptly. His nose wiggled and he sniffed. A faint, sour smell lay on the air. He turned and sniffed again. It was stronger now. He stiffened. "Jupe," he called. "You, Jupe! Here! Copperheads! Here, Jupe, copperheads! Git 'em, boy!"

The dog circled the boy, nosing carefully, a deep growl rumbling in his throat. His ruff was stiff on his neck and his mouth snarled, leaving his teeth bare and white. Carefully he moved, circling, tightening the circle every round. The boy stood motionless, only his eyes following the dog. "Git him, Jupe," he whispered. "Git him!"

Suddenly the dog pounced and then jerked his head high, his front paws stiff against the ground. The boy saw the white teeth bury themselves in the snake's neck and watched while the dog flung the snake from side to side. "Good, Jupe," he said. "Good dog."

He leaned against the tree and felt a little sick. A copperhead allus did skeer him. The dog finished off the snake and came trotting over, tail high. There you are, he said to the boy. Not a thing to it. Just part of the day's work. If he could, he'd have dusted off his paws. The boy bent and hugged him. "Good dog. Good dog."

They came clear of the woods on the rutted, dusty road that saddled the hogback of the ridge. The boy plopped his feet in the dust, squeezing it up between his toes, squirming over its heat. The dog lagged behind, his tail drooping. The road was noon-hot, heavy and long. The boy switched idly with his stick at the weeds, spraying the thick powder of dust that lay on them into the air. He sneezed and threw the stick away. Wish it wasn't so fur home, he thought.

Dinner smokes were tailing out of the cabin chimneys when they came around the bend upon a crew of men working by the side of the road. There were tall poles lying in the field and a great roll of wire was heaped to one side. The boy's eyes widened and he edged toward the men.

They were digging a deep hole in the ground and one of the men was painting the end of the pole with something that smelled sharp and tangy. It turned the pole black. Nearer and nearer the boy inched. Another man had some queer-looking thing strapped on his legs. It had spikes on it.

"Hi, sonny," the man painting the pole called.

The boy ducked his head in an agony of shyness and wiggled his toes. He noticed the patches on the knees of his overalls and felt shame for them.

"Cat's got his tongue, I reckon," the man said to the one beside him.

"Hit's not!" The boy spoke sharply.

"Well, now, that's more like it. You live on this ridge road?"

The boy nodded. " 'Bout a mile on down the road." His curiosity conquered his shyness. "Watcha doin', mister? With them poles an' that thar wire an' stuff? Watcha gonna do with 'em?"

The man laughed. "Why, we're laying the electric line. You're going to have electricity back here in these hills. You know what electricity is?"

Again the boy nodded and a startled, eager look swept over his face. "I seen the 'lectric lights in the store over at the Gap oncet. Air we gonna have lights like them thar?"

"You sure are. In about two weeks we'll be ready to turn 'em on for you. You go to school?"

"Yes. Down at Spout Springs."

"Well, you can do your studying by a good light in just about two more weeks. No more coal-oil lamps here on Hickory Ridge. How'll you like that?"

But the boy was making tracks down the road, spinning a dusty cloud from his heels.

All the way home he ran, and raced through his own front yard. He flung the screen door wide and tore through the house to the kitchen. "Ma," he called. "Hey, Ma! The 'lectric's comin' to the ridge! Ma, the 'lectric's comin'."

His mother was dishing up dinner, and the fire from the wood stove in the corner of the cook room had laid a steamy blanket over the house. The woman wiped sweat from her face with the tail of her apron and pushed at a straggling lock of hair with the back of her hand. The boy pulled at her dress. "Ma? Didja hear me? Ma, the 'lectric's comin'. I seen the men aputtin' up the poles down the road apiece. An' they said hit'd be ready in about two weeks."

"Go shet the screen, Jeff. Hit's hung up an' the flies'll be aswarmin' in."

Impatiently the boy ran back and pulled the door to. "Won't it be somethin' now, to have lights like them over at the Gap, Ma? Jist think. Nice an' brightlike. An' I seen John Barry light 'em oncet an' all he done was turn somethin' an' they come on. Just a little ole thing he turned an' they was bright light like daytime."

The boy whirled and flicked an imaginary switch. "Snick," he said, and ran through the three rooms of the house, flicking switches in every room. "Snick," he said. "Jist like that. See, Ma, the lights is on."

The woman laid a hand to the small of her back and straightened. "Wash up, Jeff. Yer pa's comin' in now an' dinner's ready."

The boy hopped around the room, three steps on one foot, three steps on the other. "Oh, hippety-hip, skippety-skip. Oh, snickety-snick an' spickety-spick. Snick, lights on. Snick, lights off. Snick, lights on." He whirled and danced around the room.

The man came in and hung his shattered straw hat on a nail by the wash shelf. He eyed the boy as he poured water in the tin basin. "What ails him?"

The woman poured clabber-milk in thick, white cups. "The 'lectric's comin'."

The man ran a snaggle-toothed comb through his sparse hair. "So?" He put the comb back in its rack. "Set down, Jeff, an' quit that prancin' 'round. We ain't got the 'lectric yit."

"But we *will* have, Pa. I seen the men aworkin' down the road. They was puttin' up the poles, an' they had wire an' little glass cups an' ever'thing ready. An' they said hit wouldn't be but two weeks till they could turn it on." The boy slid along the bench back of the table.

The man heaped his plate and fell to eating. The woman waved a sassafras branch at the flies and heaped the boy's plate. "Eat yer dinner," she said.

On Monday when the boy went to school the talk was all of the electric. "I seen 'em," he boasted to the other boys. "Me an' Jupe was sang diggin' a Sattidy, an' we seen 'em acomin' home. They was puttin' up the poles."

"I seen 'em, too."

"Me too."

"I bet I seen 'em first," Jeff insisted.

"Naw, you never. I seen 'em when they was crossin' the holler over by Crooked Creek. We're a-aimin' to have the lights, an' Ma says she's agonna have her a washin' machine an' a 'lectric iron." This was Willie Price, a tall, freckled, gangly boy.

"You all aimin' to have the 'lectric, Jeff?"

"Why, shore," the boy said. "Hit's acomin' right by our house."

Each day after school the boy went to watch the men. They crept down the road a few poles each day. The boy watched them string the wires into the houses along the way and waited impatiently for them to reach his house. He counted the days.

"You'll soon be to my house," he told the men one day. "Hit's the next un 'round the bend."

"The next one?" one of the men asked.

The boy nodded. "Next un jist 'round the bend."

The men looked at each other and went on working. One man dug his shovel into the ground fast and hard. "You'll break that thar shovel," the boy cautioned. "You hadn't ort to gouge it so hard." The man grunted and swung the dirt in a wide arc.

That night the boy told his mother, "Tomorrer they'll be to our house. They're jist around the bend. They'll git here tomorrer."

Tomorrow was another Saturday and the boy stayed all day with the men, Jupe hanging around on the edge. About noon the men set the pole directly in front of the house. But when the pole was set the men went on down the road. Jeff was puzzled. At all the other houses they had strung wire to the side of the house. They didn't do that at his house. Well, maybe they was goin' to eat an' was comin' back later.

He went in to dinner. "They got our pole up now," he told his mother. "But they ain't strung our wire yit. Likely they'll git to 'fore night, though." He dried his hands carefully on the feed sack they used for a towel and slid behind the table.

His mother waved at the flies. "We ain't gonna have the 'lectric, Jeff. Hit costes money to git yer house fixed fer it an' it costes three dollars ever' month to the light company. We cain't be spendin' for sich."

The boy's eyes were unbelieving. "But hit's right thar on the pole," he said. "Hit's jist right outside. They said we'd have lights in two weeks. They *said* it, Ma."

"They ain't the ones going to pay fer havin' the house fixed fer it, an' they ain't the ones to pay the three dollars ever' month, neither. We ain't gonna have the 'lectric, Jeff, an' that's all they is to it. You'll jist have to make up yer mind to it. We ain't got the money."

The boy pushed his plate back. His stomach fluttered like it had little butterflies in it, and he couldn't touch his food. They wasn't goin' to have the 'lectric. Why, they jist had to have it! Why, thar it was! Right outside the front yard! Snick, lights on. Snick, lights off. Oh, they jist had to have the 'lectric. Ever'-body else would be havin' it an' they'd be onliest ones 'thout it. Hit wasn't to be borne they shouldn't have it.

A knot stuck in his throat and hurt him all through and his chest felt heavy so that he couldn't get a good breath. Oh, hit wasn't to be thought of. Why, he'd been the first to see 'em puttin' in the poles. He jist knowed Willie Price had lied when he said he seen 'em over on Crooked Creek. Hit was him seen 'em first. An' they was goin' to turn it on, come Tuesday. All up and down the ridge the lights would go on. All at one bright, beautiful moment they'd go on. Jist Jeff Tabor's house would be dark. Jist his'n of 'em all. The lights'd be asparklin' like candles on a Christmas tree, so purty an' daytime-like. Ever house'd be lit up, come Tuesday. Ever' house but his'n. One small tear ran down his nose. He shook it off and blinked into his cup of milk. He couldn't swallow a drop. Hit jist wouldn't go down.

Suddenly he brightened, eager and hopeful. "You could have my sang money, Ma," he said. "I've got nearabouts ten dollars, an' likely three dollars more of them roots I got last time." Maybe they could have the 'lectric for a few months anyway.

"Hit costes clost to fifty dollars jist to wire the house, Jeff," the woman said. "Yore sang money'd jist be a drap in the bucket."

The boy's heart chunked down to his stomach again. He shoved the bench back against the wall and wandered through the house to the front porch. He wrapped his arm around a post and leaned his head against it. Hit wasn't right. Why was it, on the whole endurin' ridge they was the onliest ones couldn't have the 'lectric? Why was it they was allus the ones had to do without? Make do with a ole blind mule when ever'body else had a good team? Made do with a ole rusty step-stove to cook on, when ever'body else had a good black range with warmin' ovens? Make do with homemade overalls when ever'body else had boughton ones? Hit jist wasn't right, somehow. The lump came up in his throat again and came out in a sob. He turned his head against the post and let the salt tears flow unheeded.

Monday came and went. The boy was quiet at school, saying no more about the 'lectric. The excitement ran high. "Tomorrer's the day," the others shouted. "Tomorrer's when they turn the 'lectric on. Hey, Jeff, we got a light in ever' room. Even in the loft room. You all git lights fer all yer rooms?"

Jeff turned away. Tomorrer they'd know the Tabors didn't git the 'lectric. Tomorrer when all the lights went on they'd know. He wished he hadn't come to school today. He wished he could go 'way off in the woods an' stay till after tomorrer. Jist him and Jupe. So they wouldn't have to see the lights, an' see ever'body aknowin' the Tabors didn't have the 'lectric. He couldn't bear today and tomorrer.

But he did, drooping quietly through the hours. Mebbe the sun wouldn't come up on Tuesday. Mebbe he'd sleep all day an' not have to go to school. Mebbe, if he waked up and went outside there'd be the wires arunnin' to their house after all. Mebbe somethin' could happen yit.

But the sun came up and Jeff waked early and when he went outside the pole stood there, lonely and bare. No wires stretching to the house. A thin, bilious saliva flooded the boy's mouth and he swallowed hard. Hit was jist goin' to hafta be, then. They wasn't nothin' goin' to change it. The Tabors jist wasn't going to have the 'lectric. An' the kids at school would snicker an' whisper behind their backs an' say again what they'd said before about Poke Tabor bein' a do-less man an' how his hands fit a fishin' pole better'n they fit a plow handle. Hit was jist goin' to hafta be.

He left his breakfast untouched, but he took his lunch bucket when his mother handed it to him and he set out doggedly for school. Jupe trailed behind, perplexed and saddened by the boy's quietness.

"Hit'll be at seven tonight," the boys said. "Seven on the dot the men said. Jist at first dark they'll turn it on."

"We done got ever' light turned on an' ready," Willie Price said. "When they turn it on, they'll all be lit up at oncet."

Jeff doubled up his fist. He'd like to hit that thar Willie Price right on the nose. Allus abraggin', he was.

The day moved on and the teacher finally called, "Books away." Jeff lingered behind so as not to have to listen to the talk goin' up the ridge. Jupe was waiting for him outside and the boy rubbed his nose against the dog's thick fur. "Jupe," the boy whispered. "Oh, Jupe!" The dog licked his tongue over the boy's nose and whimpered. This trouble the boy was bearing, maybe he could lick it away.

The sun slid down behind the ridge and the first whippoorwills began to call. The cow belled her way across the pasture and the boy and the dog went to drive her to the barn. Hit would be soon, now. Soon. Dark was alayin' over the trees, an' the night dew was risin' fast. The boy wet his feet in the grass as he went toward the house. If I jist didn't hafta see 'em, he thought. If I could jist go to bed an' things'd be like allus. If I jist didn't hafta know about it.

His mother called him to supper. As they sat down she lit the lamp. Dimly it glowed over the table, flickering small shadows around the room. The boy choked and bent his head. Now was the time. Now, hit was there. Hit wasn't to be borne.

"Reckon the other lamp'd give more light," the woman said, "but I'm too tard to git it."

The boy looked at the small flame; then suddenly his young face set in determination. He jumped up and took the lamp into the other room, setting it on the table near the window. Quickly he took the lamp on the mantelpiece and lit it, and he set it on the table, too. He went into the back room and brought the biggest lamp they hardly ever used because it took so much oil, and he lit it and set it beside the other lamps. Now. Now, they was all lit and they made a bright, soft light. They glowed all through the room and they showed through the window onto the porch outside. They showed plumb down to the road, bright and gleaming. They was almost like the 'lectric.

He went out and sat in the grass of the yard and pulled his knees up to his chin and looked at the light. The dog nuzzled him and rested his head on the boy's shoulder. Absently the boy pulled the dog's ears. He felt sad and a little lonesome, as if he'd gone someplace and left something good and sweet behind. He'd like to have it back. He felt a little lost without it, but he sensed dimly it was gone forever.

"O' course, Jupe," he told the dog, a small sigh slipping out, "o' course Ma ain't goin' to let us burn the lamps ever' night. Hit would be a pure waste of oil. But someday, Jupe." He hugged the dog fiercely. "Someday the lights is goin' to be on ever' night at the Tabors'. Don't you grieve, Jupe, an' don't you fret. Jist wait an' 'fore you know it . . ."

He buried his face in the dog's neck. "I cain't take you fishin' no more, Jupe, for I cain't take the chance of gittin' my hands to fit a fishin' pole. Fish don't git you no money. An' I cain't take you sang diggin' no more, fer sang don't git you enough money. You got to plow to git money. You got to plow terbaccer an' corn to git money. You've not ever thought about gittin' money, Jupe, but you got to git used to it. You've jist gone to school an' gone fishin' an' dug sang an' hunted squirrels. But they ain't gonna be no more o' that, Jupe. Commencin' tomorrer we got to plow. Gittin' money is the biggest thing they is an' commencin' tomorrer we're aimin' to git it."

He stretched out on the grass, pillowing his head on the dog's flanks. His fingers snapped and he laughed. "Won't be no time . . . won't be no time till all we got to do is, snick, lights on—snick, lights off. Won't be no time."

The dog whispered in his throat and curled and rested his muzzle against the boy's face.

Then the lights went out and the boy and the dog slept in the dark.

Caroline Gordon

THE BRILLIANT LEAVES

At three o'clock he came out of the gallery. His mother and his aunt were at the far end, knitting. He had half an hour to kill and he stood, leaning against a post and listening to their talk. They liked to sit there in the afternoons and gossip about all the people who had come to this summer resort in the last thirty years. The Holloways—he was the grandson of a South Carolina bishop and she allowed her children to go barefooted and never attended vesper services; that Mrs. Paty who had had a fit one day in the post office; the mysterious boarder who came every summer to the Robinsons. They knew them all. They were talking now about something that had happened a long time ago. A girl named Sally Mainwaring had climbed down a rope ladder to meet her sweetheart while her father stood at another window, shotgun in hand. When she got to the ground the lover had scuttled off into the bushes, "and so," his aunt concluded dramatically, "she came back into the house through the front door and was an old maid the rest of her life."

"Those Mainwaring girls were all fast," his mother said reflectively.

"Not fast, Jenny, wild."

"High-spirited," his mother conceded. "Come to think of it, Sally Mainwaring was the first woman I ever saw ride astride. I remember. I was about ten years old and she came by the house on a big black horse. I thought about Queen Elizabeth reviewing the troops at Banbury."

"Tilbury, Jenny. You always get things wrong."

"Tilbury or Banbury," his mother said. "It's all one. Kate, do you throw over a stitch here or just keep on purling?"

He had his watch open in his hand and now he snapped it shut and stepped off the gallery onto the ground. His mother looked up quickly. "Aren't you going to play tennis this afternoon, Jimmy?"

"No," he said. "I thought I'd just take a turn in the woods," and he was gone up the path before she could speak again.

The path took him quickly into the woods. The mountain arched up its western brow here and it was all wooded, but the cottage—the cottage to which his family had come every summer since he was born—was on an open slope facing north. When you stood on the gallery and looked out, you had the roofs of all those little white houses spread below you. He halted once imperceptibly and glanced back. They always looked just alike, those houses. He wondered how his mother and his aunt could sit there every afternoon talking about the people who lived in them.

He took his watch out again. "Meet me at half past three," Evelyn had said. It was only ten minutes past now. He didn't want to get there first and just stand waiting. He slowed his pace. This part of the woods he was in now was full of black gums. The ground under his feet was red with the brilliant, fallen leaves. "Spectacular," his aunt called it. He had come here yesterday on a duty walk with her and with his mother. His aunt kept commenting on the colors of the leaves, and every now and then she would make him pick one up for her. "The entrance to the woods is positively spectacular," she told everybody when she got home.

All the time he had been wondering when Evelyn would get there. And then this morning her letter had come. ". . .We're leaving Friday morning. I've got to get up in a minute and start packing. . . ."

He said over to himself the part about the train. "I'm telling you which one it is, but don't come to meet it. Don't even come to the house—first. I'll meet you at our tree. I can be there by half past . . ."

He came to a log and, standing flat-footed, jumped over it. When he landed on the other side he broke into a run, hands held chest high, feet beating the ground in a heavy rhythm, the kind of stride you used in track. He ran four or five hundred yards then stopped, grinning and looking about him as if there might have been somebody there to see.

Another five hundred yards carried him to the tree. Evelyn was already there, walking up and down, her hands in the pockets of her brown sweater. She heard him, turned and came running, so fast that they bumped into each other. She recoiled but he caught her to him and held her awkwardly until he had pressed his mouth on hers. Her lips, parting beneath his, felt firm and cool, not warm and soft as they had been when they kissed good-by in June under this same tree.

His arm was still about her, but she was pulling away to look up into his face."Dimmy!" she said.

They both laughed because that was what his aunt called him sometimes and it made him mad. Then they drew apart and started walking down the road. Her brown hair was long, now, and done up in a knot, and she had on Girl Scout shoes and bright red socks and she kept scuffling the leaves up as she went. He walked beside her, his hands in his pockets. Now that he didn't have his arms around her he felt awkward.That was because she was silent, like the picture he had at home on his dresser, not laughing and talking or turning her head the way she really did.

She looked up at him, sidewise. "It's different, isn't it?" she said.

His impulse was to stop short but he made himself walk on. He spoke and was surprised to find his voice so deep. "Why is it different, Evelyn?"

Color burned in her smooth cheek. She fixed bright, shy eyes on his. "*Silly!*" she said.

He thought that he must have sounded silly. Still she didn't have any business to say what she had. His face hardened. "Why is it different?" he persisted in the same controlled voice.

She jumped up, high enough to snatch a wine-colored leaf from the bough over her head. "Everything was green, then," she said. "Last time we were here the woods were just turning green."

He remembered the June woods. His face, which some people thought too heavy, lightened. "I know a place where it's still green," he said. "I was there the other day. There's some yellow leaves but it's mostly green. Like summer."

"Come on," she said and caught his extended hand. They raced down the road, scattering the brilliant leaves from under their feet. After a little they came out on the brow of the mountain. There was no red carpet there. What trees could be seen, stunted hackberries mostly, grew in crevices of the rock. They went forward and stood on the great ledge that was called Sunset Point. Below them the valley shimmered in autumn haze. They could see the Murfreesboro road cutting its way through fields of russet sedge, or suddenly white against a patch of winter oats. They watched a black car spin along past the field and disappear into the tunnel of woods that marked the base of the mountain. Suddenly she stretched her arms out and tilted her head back so that she was looking straight into the sky. "The sky's on fire," she cried and laughed out loud like a child.

He touched her arm. "Let's go down there," he said and pointed to the road which wound along the side of the ledge.

They stepped over the drift of dead leaves which choked the entrance and started down. The road slanted steeply along the mountainside. The boughs of the trees met over it in some places. Frail grass grew in the ruts and there were ferns along the edge. What sun got through lay in bright coins on the frail grass and the ferns. The air was cool, not with autumn chill but with the coolness of the deep shade.

The rock they sat down on was tufted with moss. She laid her hand on it, fingers outspread and curving downward. "Look," she said, "every one's like a little pine tree."

"Sometimes they have little flowers on them," he said.

He watched the slim, tanned fingers sink deeper among the little green sprays. "I thought you might not come today," he said. "I heard the train and I thought maybe you didn't come."

"We almost didn't," she said. "Mother got a telegram at the last minute."

"Who from?"

"Aunt Sally Mainwaring. She's always coming to see us."

"Is that the old lady that stays at the Porters'?"

She nodded indifferently. "She's awful crabby."

"I heard mother and my aunt talking about her. They said she climbed out of a window to elope."

She nodded again. "But he was gone when she got down there, so she was an old maid. That's what makes her so crabby."

They both laughed. Off in the woods a bird called, an unbearably sweet note that seemed to belong to summer rather than autumn. She was looking at the road where it disappeared around a great boulder whose base was thick with ferns. "Where does it go?"

"To Cowan. They call it the old Confederate road. My grandfather came along here once."

"What for?"

"I don't know," he answered vaguely. "He said it was a night attack."

She had got up and was moving over to the place where the ferns grew most luxuriantly. She stood and looked down at them. "Just like summer," she said. "It's just like summer in here, isn't it, Jimmy?"

"Yes, it is," he said.

She walked on. He followed her around the corner of the great boulder. "Have you been playing much tennis?" she asked.

"There wasn't anything else to do," he said.

"How's your backhand?"

"Pretty good. There was a new fellow here this summer could beat me two out of three."

"That Jerrold boy from Atlanta?"

"How'd you know about him?"

"Pinky Thomas wrote me."

He was silent. He had not known that she corresponded with Pinky Thomas. "I don't reckon I'll be playing so much tennis from now on," he said at length.

She made no comment. He leaned down and pulled some beggar's lice from his trouser leg. "I don't reckon I'll be up here much next summer. Not more'n two weeks anyhow. You lay off all summer and it shows on you all right. But I don't reckon that makes much difference."

"Why won't you be up here next summer?" she asked in a low voice.

"Dad wants me to go in his office," he said. "I reckon I better start. I suppose—I suppose if you're ever going to make a living you better get started at it."

She did not answer, then suddenly she stepped up on the edge of the rock. He jumped up beside her. "Evelyn," he said, "would you marry me?"

She was looking off through the woods. "They wouldn't let us," she said; "we're too young."

"I know," he said, "but if I go in dad's office. I mean . . . pretty soon I'd get a raise. I mean . . . you would, wouldn't you?"

She turned her head. Their eyes met. Hers were a light, clear brown like the leaves that lie sometimes in the bed of a brook. "I'm perfectly *crazy* about you," she said.

He lifted her in his arms and jumped from the rock. They sank down in the bed of ferns. When he kissed her she kissed him back. She put her arms around his neck and laid her cheek against his, but when he slipped his hand inside the V of her sweater to curve it into the soft hollow under her arm she drew away. "Don't," she said, "please, Jimmy."

"I won't," he said.

She let him kiss her again, then she got to her knees. He sat up straight beside her and caught her hand and held it tight. Her hand fluttered in his then broke away. "It's still in here," she said. "No, it isn't, either. I hear running water."

"It's the falls," he said. "Bridal Veil Falls is round the corner of that big ledge."

"I never have seen it," she said.

"It's not very pretty around there," he said.

She was laughing and her eyes had more than ever that look of leaves in a running brook. "I bet it's prettier than it is here," she said.

He stood up, straightened his tie and passed a hand over his hair then stretched a hand out to her. She jumped up beside him lightly. "It's this way," he said and struck off on a path through the ferns. She followed close. Sometimes they could walk side by side. Sometimes when he had to go in front he put his hand back and she held on to it.

He stopped abruptly beside a big sycamore. She was walking fast and ran into him. He embraced her and kissed her, hard. "You're so sweet," he whispered.

She said again, "I'm *crazy* about you," and then she pulled away to look up at him. "Don't you—don't you like doing things together, Jimmy?"

"Some things," he said and they laughed and after that stepped side by side for a while.

They came out of the hollow and were on the brow of the mountain again. In front of them was a series of limestone ledges that came down one after another like steps. Gushing out from one of them, filling the whole air with the sound of its rushing, was the white waterfall they called the Bridal Veil.

She drew her breath in sharply. "I never was here before," she cried.

He led her past one of the great boulders which were all about them. They set their feet on the ledge from which the water sprang.

"Look," he said, "you can see where it comes out." She leaned forward in the curve of his arm. The water came down out of a fissure in the highest ledge. It was pure and colorless at first, but it whitened as it struck the first rock step. She leaned farther forward, still with his arm curving about her. Far below were a few pools of still water, fringed with ferns, but most of the water kept white with its dashing from ledge to ledge. She turned quickly, and he felt the cold drops of moisture as her cheek brushed his. "It is like a bridal veil," she said.

He was eyeing the great shelf that made the first falls. "There's a place in there where you can stand and be dry as a bone," he said.

"Have you been there?"

He nodded. "Bill Thompson and I climbed through once. Long time ago. We must have been about ten years old."

She was still turned away from the water, facing him. Her eyes brightened. "Would you do it again?" she asked.

He hesitated, conscious of his body that seemed now to belong more to the ground than it had eight years ago. "I reckon I could if I had to," he said.

Her fingers closed on his arm. "Let's do it now."

He stared at her. "Are you crazy?" he asked.

She did not answer. Her face was bent down. He could see that her eyes were traveling along the main ledge. "How did you go?" she asked.

He pointed to a round rock that rose in the middle of the shelf. "We climbed up over that and then when you get back in there it's like a little path."

Her fingers were softly opening and closing on his arm. She reached up suddenly and gave his cheek a feather-like touch. "I *like* doing things together," she said.

He was looking at her steadily. The color had risen in his cheeks. Suddenly he bent and began untying her shoe-laces. "You'll have to take these off if you're going along there," he said.

She stood on one foot and drew off, one after another, shoes and socks. He took his own shoes off and tied them around his neck, then slung hers around, too. "You're the doctor," he said. "Come on."

They climbed to the top of the round rock. He jumped down, then stood braced while she jumped beside him. They stood there and looked down the great black staircase. She squeezed his arm and then she leaned out a little way over the ledge. "Look how the ferns follow the water all the way down," she said.

"Don't try to see too much," he told her and made her straighten up. They stepped carefully along the ledge over the place that he had said was like a little path. The falls were not three feet away, now. He could feel the cold spray on his cheek, could see the place under the water where you could stand and be dry. "Come on," he said. "One more rock to get around."

The second rock did not jut out as far as the other, but the rock under their feet was wet and a little slippery in places. He thought he would go first and then he decided he could help her better from his side. "Go easy," he said.

She stepped lightly past him. He saw her foot go out and her body swing around the rock and then—he never knew. She might have slipped or she might have got scared, but her foot went down, sickeningly, and she was falling backward from the rock. He clutched at her and touched only the smooth top of her head. Her face was before him, thrown sharply backward, white, with staring eyes—and then he had to lean out to see, lying far below among the ferns—the brown heap.

He got down there—he never could tell them afterward what way he took—but he got down there, slipping, sliding, over the wet rocks. She was lying by one of those little pools on her back, her brown hair tangled in the ferns. He knelt beside her. "Evelyn," he said, "are you hurt? Are you hurt very bad?" Her eyes were open but she did not answer except for a moan. He bent over farther, put his hand on her shoulder. "Could you stand up?" he asked. "Oh, darling, couldn't you just stand up?" The moaning sound went on and now he knew that she did not see him and he started up, his hands swinging at his sides. Then he knelt down again and tried to lift her up. She screamed twice horribly. He laid her back. The screaming had stopped. He could hear the water rushing down onto the rocks. He passed his hand over his trembling lips. "I got to get some help," he said.

He said that but he took another step toward her before he turned away. His hands, still hanging at his sides, danced as though he were controlling invisible marionettes. He stared at the gray mountain ledge. "I reckon this is the way," he said and started upward, stumbling over the wet rocks.

Fifteen minutes later he came up over the top of the ledge onto the western brow. One of his trouser legs was torn off and blood showed through the fluttering rags of his shirt. He stood on the ledge and put his hand up and wiped the sweat from his forehead and shut his eyes for a second. Then he plunged into the underbrush. A few more minutes and he came out onto the woods road. He ran slower now, lurching sometimes from side to side, but he ran on. He ran and the brilliant, the wine-colored leaves crackled and broke under his feet. His mouth, a taut square, drew in, released whining breaths. His starting eyes fixed the ground, but he did not see the leaves that he ran over. He saw only the white houses that no matter how fast he ran kept always just ahead of him. If he did not hurry they would slide off the hill, slide off and leave him running forever through these woods, over these dead leaves.

A.B. Guthrie, Jr.

EBBIE

Ebony, the Gordon setter, was in heat again, and a bunch of dogs always were hanging around the Bostwick house. From the window Charlie could see the Jacksons' yellow cur, Tip, and the bulldog that the Johnsons had sent east for and the Bowmars' little Sprite and four or five others, some of which he wasn't sure of. Sometimes they fought, but not often. Mostly they were friendly and patient, lying with their tongues hanging out and their eyes on the back door, or one after the other cocking their legs against the old cottonwood tree or the ax-marked chopping block that Father cut firewood on.

Because old Eb was in heat, Father was out of humor with her. Coming home from the office and seeing all the dogs lying around, he walked stiff and kept his eyes on the ground as if Eb was bringing shame on the house. It was the same in the morning when he set out for work and maybe found Tip lying just outside the door. He would aim a sudden kick at him and go on while words sounded in his throat.

Charlie didn't know what made Father feel that way. Grown-ups had reasons of their own that you wouldn't understand until you were grown up yourself. Until then you didn't ask and you didn't object; you just wondered, like wondering why Father sometimes was full of play and tricks, and it was like the sun shining inside the house, and then at other times, for no cause that a boy could understand, he was touchy and short-tempered, and it was like a thundercloud had come across the sun.

Charlie sat down on the floor and let his hand run over the thick, curl of Eb's coat. She was tipped with gold, but most of her was watered black. She looked at him, out of her good eye, and her tail made a slow pat on the floor. The other eye had been put out by birdshot long ago, before Charlie could remember. There was just the hole there and the lids half-closed and the meat showing a little behind them and always a little wet streak down her muzzle where the eye drained. Father said he had tried to dust her, when they were out hunting, because she ranged too far, and one of the shot had happened to get in her eye.

Eb loved Father, maybe understanding him better than a boy could. She loved the smell of his hunting jacket and the sound his shotgun made as he tried the pump before setting out for prairie chickens or mallards or geese. She would prance crazily around him and whine almost like talking and he would smile and say, "All right, old girl. All right."

Father said maybe Eb didn't have the best nose in the world, but he would like to see her equal at retrieving. She would go anywhere to get his birds and bring them and lay them at his feet without a tooth mark on them. Charlie thought she must have a pretty good nose at that or she wouldn't find anything at all, not with just one good eye. He would try her out himself as soon as he was old enough to carry a gun. He felt old enough now, at nine years, but Mamma said he would have to wait until he was twelve at least. So all he could do was play with Eb. He had broken her to lead and to pull a wagon, and she would scratch like everything for him, trying to dig a gopher out. He bet that next to hunting she liked to be with him best, tagging at his heels or retrieving the sticks he threw or just lying with him behind the big range in the kitchen where the slow warmth sometimes put them both to sleep.

Outside, the day was dimming off toward dark. The dogs were all lying down, some of them with their eyes closed but with their ears alive and listening. Father was probably on his way home by now.

Charlie got up and put on his sweater and went to the kitchen to go outside. His mother turned from her work board, the ends of her fingers lumpy with dough and smiled at him. She said, "Don't go far. It'll be suppertime before long."

"I'm just going out."

"What for?"

"Well, I thought—you see, Father doesn't like the dogs in the yard, and I thought—"

She turned back to the board, and it was a little time before she spoke. Then she said, "I see, dear. Watch Eb doesn't go out with you."

Eb tried to follow him, her heavy brush of tail wagging hopefully, but he kneed her back and closed the door. He had stored a handful of rocks by the step, and now he picked them up, yelled, "Get out of here!" and began pegging the stones at the dogs, throwing easy and not very straight. The dogs slid out of range and stopped and grinned at him.

Father was silent at the supper table, thinking thoughts and feeling things Charlie couldn't guess. Once he asked, "Where's Eb?" and Mamma answered, "On the back porch. I latched the door," and Father went on eating and thinking. The porch was boarded up for three feet or so and screened the rest of the way to the top.

It had grown darker, so dark you couldn't see out the window from the lighted room, but Charlie knew the dogs had come back. He knew it even before he heard the sounds of the fight. Father's face clouded. "Those dogs!"

It was Mamma who found later that Eb had got out. She opened the door to the porch and turned back and stood with a still and startled look on her face, and the knowledge of what had happened leaped up in Charlie and clutched his insides. He started to whisper, "I'll find her," but Father came into the kitchen just then and caught the still and startled look, too, and asked, "What's wrong?" and looked outside and saw where Eb had made a hole through the screen.

Father went over to the corner where Charlie had leaned his ball bat and picked it up and said, "Come along, son! You can help locate her."

Two up-and-down lines marked Mamma's forehead, between the eyes. "Please, Harold," she said, and added, "It's just natural," but Father acted as if he didn't hear her. He slammed through the screen door with the bat held tight in his hand.

They found Eb right away, at the rear of the vacant lot next to their house. To Charlie it seemed there must have been a hundred dogs around. Some of them were just shapes at the edge of darkness. One was on top of Eb. Father ran up, waving the bat. It was the Jackson's dog, Tip, that was on top. Father swung at him and missed, and Tip leaped off and jumped away and stood waiting, his eyes sharp and his mouth open and his hanging tongue looking dark in the half-dark.

Father grabbed Eb by the collar and started jerking her back toward the house. When his back was turned, Tip ran up again and rose on his hind legs and began hugging Eb with his front ones. Eb hung back, and Father turned and saw what was happening and swung the bat at Tip and, after he had missed again, raised it high and brought it down on Eb's head. The solid whack of it was drowned out by the howl that burst out of Eb. It was a high, shrill, wavy howl that hurt the ears like a whistle, and it went on and on, not stopping even for a breath.

Father jerked her ahead again and dragged her up the steps and flung her toward the rag rug on the porch. Then he moved the wood box over so that it covered the hole she had made in the screen. "She won't want to be getting out again this night, I'm thinking," he said in a voice that made Charlie's stomach draw up.

Mamma looked at him when they came in the house, and Father said, still in that hard, ungiving tone, "I made a dead dog out of my dog, almost." Eb's crying reached inside the house. It sounded a little weaker here, but it still hurt the ears and it still went on and on as if the pain in her never let up even for a swallow or a gulp of air.

Mamma's voice was so quiet it made Charlie look at her. "I don't know why you let yourself get into these blind rages. You've made a dog out of yourself, I'm afraid." Charlie saw that her face was white and that the hands over the dishpan trembled. He never had heard her speak to Father that way before, and he drew back inside himself, expecting a fierce answer, but Father didn't say a word. He turned and walked from the room.

"You get ready for bed, son," Mamma said, not looking at him.

Before he went to school the next morning, Charlie found what had made Eb howl. He had gone to tell her goodbye, and her tail thumped on the floor for him, and she raised her old head. He held still, unbelieving, and the breath in him held still, too, while the fact beat against him. He saw the blind eye and the glimmer of red behind the lids, but what he couldn't believe he saw was the other eye, blind now, too, and empty-socketed, and the seepage from it making an unclean furrow down her nose.

He didn't cry. There were no tears in him, only a feeling of emptiness, only the feeling of unbelieving. He dropped down and brought her head into his lap and couldn't look at the eye again. "Oh, Ebbie," he whispered, "why did you have to do it? Why did you have to go and do it, Ebbie?" She let her head rest in his lap, and her tail wagged on as always, but slower, Charlie thought, than he had ever seen it.

Mamma called from inside, "You'll be late for school, Charlie," and he got up, not answering, and picked up his books and made his feet take him away. He couldn't tell anyone what had happened, not even Mamma. He had to hold it tight inside himself, a cold secret that lay in his stomach like a weight all day.

Coming back after school, he saw the dogs in the back yard again, and a sudden fury came on him. He gathered up a big handful of rocks and sneaked up and began throwing hard and straight as he could, feeling a fierce biting inside his chest when one of the stones brought a yelp from Tip.

Inside, he still couldn't tell Mamma about Eb, though he wondered if the knowing of it wasn't what made her quiet and gentler, even, than usual. He refused the cookies she offered and afterward stole out to the porch. It was true. The secret was true. He got Eb's head in his lap again.

Father was late getting home. The sun had gone beyond the mountains and the light was fading out of things before Charlie heard his step. Charlie slipped into the bathroom, leaving the door open just a crack, not wanting to see Father now, not wanting Father to see his face and read the secret in it. The front door opened and closed, and Charlie heard the rustle of clothing as Father took off his topcoat. He heard Mamma coming from the kitchen and then her voice, sounding low but not sharp, sounding low and gentle. "Ebbie's blind, Harold. Her other eye's out. I don't know what to tell Charlie. Maybe he knows already." The voice faltered before it got through.

There was a long silence. In his mind Charlie could see Father, standing with his head bent and his mouth set while he thought. The silence grew into a ringing in the ears, and then Father's step broke it, lagging toward the kitchen.

Mamma's voice was just above a whisper. "What are you going to do?"

"There's only one thing." Father's steps went on.

Charlie flung open the bathroom door and ran out. Mamma wasn't to the kitchen yet. She turned and said, "Charlie."

He cried out, "I know. I know. I've got to see!"

"I wish you wouldn't go."

"I've got to."

Her hand, uplifted in a little movement, stayed him for an instant. Her eyes searched his face. "Don't be angry, Charlie. Don't feel hard toward Father. Try to understand. He's sorry, sorrier than you can know."

"Why'd he do it then?"

"He couldn't help himself. Don't you see, he couldn't help himself?" He saw tears shining in her eyes and her mouth trembling.

"I got to go," he cried out again, and dodged her and ran to the kitchen.

Father was on the back porch. He had his shotgun in one hand and Eb's head held up in the other, looking to make sure, Charlie guessed, that the good eye wasn't good any more. He let the head down and took hold of the collar and said, "Come on, girl," and, turning, saw Charlie. "You stay back, son!"

"I got to see, I tell you. I got to see."

Father didn't say any more. He just breathed deep and began leading Eb off the porch. She bumped against the door frame as they went out. The dogs lying in the back yard got up and backed off, watching.

Father took Eb over to the vacant lot, almost to where they had found her yesterday. The dogs trailed after them, Tip in the lead.

Father's hand worked the pump, throwing a shell in the chamber, and Eb's tail waved at the sound of it. Charlie thought if she could see she would be prancing.

"Sit down, girl. Sit down."

She let her hindquarters down and looked up at Father out of her blind eyes, and her tail waved again. In the dusk Charlie could see the ugly furrow that the matter from her hurt eye made.

Father stepped back. The shotgun was a long time coming up. Charlie couldn't look when it was leveled. He couldn't believe he stood there in the dark waiting for the shot, waiting for Eb to be killed, waiting for this cold and awful end.

The roar of the gun shook him. It brought his head around. Eb had sunk to the ground. A little twitching was running over her body. After a minute it stopped, and Eb didn't stir at all except for one curl of hair moving to a breath of air.

Father went over to her and stooped and put his hand out and rested it on her side. He didn't speak, not for a long time, but just stooped and let his hand lie soft and kind on her side. He moved his head a little, and Charlie saw the side of his face downturned on the ground, and of a sudden it seemed to the boy he had never seen the face before, never seen the sadness there and the kindness, too, and the marks of wild, dark angers that he couldn't help.

Father's voice sounded tired. "Run to the woodshed and get the spade, will you, son?"

When Charlie hesitated, Father said, "We'll dig a grave under the Balm of Gilead. I think she'd like to lie there."

Charlie turned and ran for the woodshed, and a great sob

formed in his stomach and tore at his throat and burst out of him. He got around the corner of the shed, where Father wouldn't see him, and his legs let him down on the chopping block. He thought that all his life he would see Eb sinking to the ground and Father's sad, dark face downturned on her and the tears in Mamma's eyes. He didn't know for whom he cried, for Eb or Father or Mother or himself. He only knew, while sobs racked him and the tears streamed down his cheeks and put the taste of salt in his mouth, that now he had to cry.

Gurney Norman

THE FAVOR

Wilgus thought his grandfather seemed a whole lot slower today than usual. The old man shuffled along with his head bowed down, looking tired and a little angry. Wilgus had heard him trading sharp words with his grandmother earlier in the day. But that was a common enough thing lately. There was something about his grandfather now that was altogether uncommon, something in his tone that was as foreign to the man as all those brand-new clothes. Ordinarily he spoke in such a soft and gentle manner it was a comfort to hear his voice. But just now when he said, "Come with me to the field, Wilgus, a section of fence is down," his voice had been as heavy and nervous as it was in church when Brother Ellis called on him to pray.

And his clothes. From head to toe his grandfather had on brand-new clothes. New hat, new shoes, khaki pants with blue suspenders and a new white shirt he wore open at the collar, the sleeves rolled up to his elbows. Sometimes his grandfather dressed like that when he went to the polls to vote. But here he was, a hammer in one hand and a sack of nails in the other, sweating already, setting out in the heat of the afternoon to do a job of work. It was all so odd the normally talkative boy followed the old man to the barn without a word.

They stopped at the barn long enough to pick up a roll of wire. Then, Wilgus carrying one end, his grandfather carrying the other, side by side they walked out beyond the garden, past his grandmother's grape arbor and patch of strawberries, walked on without speaking till they rounded the bend of the hill.

But as soon as the house was out of sight behind them, the grandfather said, "Hold up a minute, Wilgus, let's rest ourselves." And he laid the wire and the hammer and nails on the ground. The old man looked all around, at the trees up the hill a ways from where they stood, then out across the narrow valley that dropped away below. He took out his handkerchief and wiped his forehead and his neck. He put the handkerchief back in his pocket, and rearranged his hat. Then he looked at his grandson and in a nervous voice confessed he hadn't brought him out to fix a fence at all.

Wilgus asked him what they'd come for, then.

"I need you to do me a favor," said the grandfather.

And he went on to tell the boy what was on his mind.

He was leaving home, he said. Going away for good. Leaving the farm, divorcing his wife, leaving Kentucky altogether, to go and live his life in another place. He wanted Wilgus to take that news to his grandma, and take some money to her he'd drawn out of the bank that morning. He reached into his pocket and brought out a roll of bills.

"Now give this to her, Wilgus. Tell her to stretch it, 'cause I've got the rest of the cash and gone with it. Oh, now, she'll scream and carry on, you might as well expect it. But it's just noise. I've stood it forty years nearly, you can stand it a minute or two. She's getting the place here. It's got a life of work in it, I reckon it ought to equal the dollars I'm taking. Anyhow it's her'n. I don't bear no grudges, tell her. She might. That's her privilege. But all my life, back and forth, pillar to post, tell her. . . ." The old man's voice trailed away then and for a moment he was silent. "Don't tell her nothing," he went on. "Just give this to her and don't tell her nothing except I'm gone."

And he counted out a hundred dollars in Wilgus' hand.

But he didn't put his roll of bills back into his pocket right away. He stood there looking thoughtfully at all the fives and tens and twenties that he held. Sucking his teeth, shaking his head dubiously, he finally peeled off another twenty and put it in the boy's hand.

"If you'll take that to your Grandma, it'll be a big help to me."

Wilgus looked at the money in his hand. "But ain't you never coming home no more?" he asked.

The grandfather quit fidgeting and for the first time that afternoon he grinned and spoke in a voice that sounded like himself. "Oh," he said. "I expect I'll see *you* again one of these days."

"But where are you going to live?"

"Well," said the grandfather. "I'm going to Floyd County for a spell. Then on over to Virginia, like as not. But I'd rather you didn't mention that to your grandma. You can keep a secret, can't you?"

Wilgus mumbled that he could. He started to ask another question, there was a lot he wanted to find out about, and to say. But somehow he couldn't get enough of it straight in his mind to form a sentence. And his grandfather seemed about out of words himself. He told Wilgus to be a good boy. Wilgus said he would. They shook hands. Then abruptly the grandfather turned and walked away, angling downhill toward the valley where the railroad was.

Wilgus took off running hard the other way.

Later, when he had his breath again, and a sense of where he was, lying on his back on the cool flat rock beside the pasture creek, Wilgus felt light in the head. It was as if he had gone to sleep when he shook hands with his grandfather, and dreamed his frantic run through trees and across a wide, steep field. Dreamed two cows had stopped their grazing to watch him running by. Dreamed his tears, dreamed the hot constriction in his chest. At one point Wilgus' lungs had felt so hot he wondered if people everywhere weren't dying because they couldn't breathe. It all might as well have been a dream, for it was fading now as he rested quietly on the rock. He felt his breathing slowly falling back to normal. He felt his heart regain its calm and easy rythm. All along his spine, the purest sense of ease that he had ever known was flowing smoothly.

Lying there, feeling the rock beneath him, hearing the water flowing past his head while overhead the leaves of the pawpaw trees brushed and flapped together, Wilgus felt something fresh inside him. Something was trying to occur to him. What was it? He didn't know. It was a feeling, a sense, that somehow this was it: everything he cared about was now at stake. In his hands. Up to him.

The question was whether or not he was up to it.

The glory was that he believed he was.

Wilgus was amazed that such a feeling was growing inside him. Suddenly his own mind awed him, he felt so powerful and so wise. All he had to do was simply lie there and it would happen. If he moved, if he stirred in the slightest, his idea would disappear before it had fully formed, and more loss than he could stand would be upon him. But if he lay still, if for once in his life he could resist his impulse to talk and do, if he could be quiet in this rare moment and give this force inside him room to grow, then all he cared about, all the things and people that he knew would be delivered, safe, and life could then go on and on and on.

Silently, now. Still.

Wilgus felt the sweat and tears drying on his skin. The creek was in slow motion just beneath his rock. Overhead the leaves of the pawpaw trees moved and rustled. Somewhere far away a solitary crow was cawing.

As long as Grandma doesn't know that Grandad's gone, it hasn't happened yet.

Wilgus sat up straight and thought: I could even sketch it if I wanted to. It would be a drawing of his grandfather getting mad and throwing something at his grandmother, a rock, a curse, a lightning bolt. And there Wilgus was, catching the bolt in his bare hands, taking the awful shock into his own body before it could strike and wound her.

With a whoop Wilgus jumped down off his rock, stripped off all his clothes and in celebration plunged into the shallow creek.

The water only came up to his knees, but by lying down and pretending, it was as good as Buckhorn Lake to him. Wilgus ducked his head and rolled and tumbled and came up spouting and splashing joyfully. His thrashing made the water muddy but when he lay still again and again grew thoughtful, the mud settled and the stream ran clear enough to drink.

As long as Grandma doesn't know it, it hasn't happened yet. She can't know if I don't tell her, and if I don't tell her she can never know.

Oh, she'll know he's *gone* all right. No preventing that. If Grandad wasn't going to live at the homeplace anymore she'd certainly know he was gone. But she didn't have to know why he was gone, what the circumstances of his leaving were. Grandad was gone, that's all. Disappeared. A mystery.

And Wilgus would become a mystery too. Oh yes. He would have to leave too, now. For his grandma's sake. To save her from the terrible thing he knew. It was a painful thing to think about but it had to be that way. For Wilgus knew that if he ever saw his grandma again he'd tell her all about Grandad leaving, tell her what he'd said. Maybe he'd even break down and tell her where he'd gone. She deserved better than that. She deserved to never know. It was a lonesome prospect, his grandfather over in Floyd County, Wilgus out on the road somewhere while his grandma lived all alone there in the house, sad old woman now. It would be tough on them all, but even so, even if they all were sad and lonely the rest of their lives, still they'd be lonely inside a web of love. At least they would have their memories of each other to be fond of. At least there still would be the past to care about.

But as Wilgus considered it, swimming and thinking in the cold creek water, the idea of going away began to seem a little severe for the way he really felt inside. Wilgus knew he couldn't live with his grandma in a daily way anymore. But perhaps he ought to stay nearby, live in walking distance of the house, secretly look in on her from time to time, keep a watch above her, do secret things to help her get along. Some mornings she'd get up and see her garden plowed, see her fruit trees pruned, her fences mended, and she would wonder: now just who on earth did that for me?

Wilgus looked around at the creek banks then, and suddenly saw how it would be. He saw the cabin he would build, a log house with mud daubed in the cracks, set back under the pawpaw trees. On the walls were animal hides, bear and coon and deer. He looked down the creek a ways to where the channel bent. There on the little bottom was where he'd have his garden. He'd drink from the creek, of course. Just below his little pool the water ran clear and pure over moss and clean, dark stones. In season wild strawberries covered the steep slope that was the pasture, and after them the blackberries came. Along the margins of the creek wild lettuce grew, and mint, and in the fall the soft pawpaws fell to the ground, as good as bananas when you're hungry.

And what the land could not provide, hard cash would. Wilgus was out of the water now, surveying his domain. He took the money out of his pocket, counted it again. That money had been ugly to him so far, a burden that weighed him down. Now it was only wealth and Wilgus ran it through his fingers, counting it again. It occurred to him to hide it, as a safeguard. As he slipped it under a certain rock he thought of the tools and equipment he would buy, the grain and the team of mules he'd use to start his homestead with.

Once the vision was complete in his mind, Wilgus put his clothes on and went to work clearing underbrush away from where the cabin was going to be. He pulled weeds and hacked at roots for over an hour. Then instead of resting he started carrying stones for the foundation and the chimney he would build. He went down to the creek's bend and in the flat place paced off his garden, thirty feet by ten. On his way back up he foraged among the rocks for mint and watercress. Then for a while he worked on his little rock dam. He'd started it earlier in the summer but hadn't got very far. Now in half an hour he did as much work as he'd done earlier in three or four days, and he would have finished it if the sun had not gone down. But it went down, a shadow passed across the water, and then it was too cold to work in the water anymore. Wilgus put his shoes on and carried chimney stones another hour. Likely he would have kept on working till after dark if suddenly the image of his grandfather had not fallen across the water at his feet.

"What are you doing, son, building yourself a town?"

The old man's sudden presence took Wilgus' breath away. Trembling, the boy let go of the rock he was lifting and stood up.

It was him, all right. It was Grandad Collier, in the flesh. And more him now than ever. The tension that had burdened his voice at noon was gone. And so were his dress-up clothes. It was just his grandfather now, wearing his familiar work clothes and his old hat, walking toward him, crossing the creek on the stones of Wilgus' dam.

"Well. You *have* been busy," said the grandfather, looking around the camp. "You move all that rock yourself?"

"I thought you went away."

The grandfather cleared his throat. "Well," he said. "I got as far as town. But I got to thinking about it. I figured I better come on back home for a while. See what happens. That all right with you?"

"But you said you was leaving home for good."

"Well, Wilgus. It's a long story. I'll tell it to you one of these days. What I'd rather talk about right now is my hundred dollars. You never spent it, did you? I notice you never took it to your grandma at the house."

Wilgus went to the hiding place and got the money.

"It's a hundred and twenty," he said.

"I tell you what," said his grandfather. "Let's call it an even hundred and ten. I'd like to give you ten dollars, for a present."

"I don't want no present."

"For wages, then. It looks to me like you've put in a pretty hard day, clearing this ground, moving all this rock around."

"Oh," said the boy. "I just been playing."

"Well," said the grandfather. "You've played hard. And you've done me a real good favor. Here." And he put the ten in the boy's pocket and made him keep it.

It was nearly dark by the time they got to where they'd left the tools and wire. And by the time they got back to the barn, full night had come. Wilgus stood outside while his grandfather went in the barn to put the tools away. Across the dark back yard he saw the lighted windows of the house. There in the kitchen was his grandmother, standing by the stove. *Grandma*, Wilgus thought. *There she is.* And when his grandfather came out of the barn and the two of them started walking together toward the house he thought: *Grandad. Here he is.* And there it was again: a feeling, deep inside, trying to occur, an idea that Wilgus would be a long time knowing. But that was okay. Let it take its time. He was a patient man. Just knowing that one day he would know was quite enough for now.

Lee Pennington

AT'S PLACE

The wind curled curious fingers around the drying October leaves where the vines ran on strings from the ground to the top of the porch and the wind produced a starchy sound scraping away the silence of late afternoon. Joe Jim's eyes followed the yellow leaf all the way down and once there it lay dead-like on the bare earth. Then he looked away, down the long narrow valley to where purple-black shadows were creeping in.

"Joe Jim, I want to talk to you."

He looked at the screen and through. She sat on the bed and he thought if he had turned just a moment earlier he would have seen her voice crawling like a thin snake through the rusty mesh.

"I know."

"Come in here where we can talk."

He shook his head yes but didn't move, his eyes now back on the yellow leaf being shoved in little jumps across the yard.

"Joe Jim, it can't wait."

"It's waited all day, ain't it?"

"It can't wait any longer. Last night I dreamed. . ." Her voice trailed off, maybe disappeared before she finished.

"You and your goddamn dreams!" He walked to the edge of the porch and stepped down; then he moved in the direction of the leaf now halfway across the yard. "Dreams," and the word was in the air, more for himself than anyone, and then gone. He stood beside the leaf. It began moving again but his foot caught it, held it, then shifted from side to side and, with his full weight pressing down, began to grind it to hundreds of little yellow pieces.

"Joe Jim?"

He heard her but was already away and toward the purple-black shadows spider weaving thin webs over the entire end of the valley.

When he returned, darkness had nearly won and all that was left to fight the great blackness was the lamp glow spilling from the window soft as fog.

"Joe Jim? Is that you?"

"It's me."

"Can we talk? We've got to work it out."

"Nothing to work out."

"Please."

He looked for shadows, pale purple shadows, but they were gone—hidden in the thick darkness covering the valley. Inside he stopped for a moment, crossed his arms in front of him, and looked at her. Her yellow hair fell smoothly and freely down and the dampness of her crying caught the lampglow gold. He shook his head side to side then crossed the room to the chair by the lamp.

"There is someone."

"No."

"Joe Jim, I know there's someone. Otherwise I wouldn't keep having these dreams."

"Don't think I ain't thought about it lately. Plenty of times!" He rubbed his hands together and stared at the ceiling, his eyes following a crack from one side to the other and back again.

"No, there's someone. I know that. A woman can feel it when it happens."

He finished rolling the cigarette and slipped his tongue slowly across the paper then sealed it. Then he held a strip of paper over the lamp waiting for the fire.

"Last night. . ."

Blue smoke rose up around, drifting first toward the lamp and rushing suddenly upward.

"What about last night?"

"Where'd you go?"

"I didn't go."

"You did. When I woke up, I called for you. You didn't answer."

He didn't answer this time either but rather watched the lamp flame forming teeth, yellow dog teeth with wiry smoke curling up from the jagged points. The wick needs trimming, he thought.

"You're not listening."

"I'm listening."

"Is she pretty?"

He began running the thumb and first finger of his left hand over his eyes, turning his head side to side. "She doesn't exist."

"Is she prettier than me?"

"I've told you. She doesn't exist. There's nobody."

"In my dreams she's just a blue haze, almost like fog on a dark morning. I can feel her and I know she's there. But I can't see her. I wish I knew what she looked like, if she's pretty."

"Those damn dreams! You've not let me near you since you started having those crazy dreams of yours. Crazy, that's all they are. Just crazy damn dreams!"

"No, they're for real. I know they're for real!"

"They're damn crazy dreams and they've got hold of you like some bright eyed devil. They won't turn you loose. They've taken over."

"Where'd you go last night?"

"Damn it to hell! I told you I didn't go anyplace."

"You went to Hindeman."

"What the hell would I go to Hindeman for?"

"To meet her. You went to meet her."

"They've taken over you completely. They're eating your heart away like maggots."

"You went to At's Place. Is there such a place in Hindeman?"

"Sure there is. It's a beer joint. But I've never been inside the place in my life."

"You were there last night, you and her."

"How many times do I have to tell you? There's no one else and I didn't go anyplace last night."

"Above the door the sign says *At's Place* and last night the wind played with it, rocked it back and forth making a screechy sound like a limb rubbing a tin roof. If I had started dreaming a minute earlier, I would have seen her. But when I started, she was already inside and you were following her through the door. Inside it was too dark for me to tell what she looked like. Is she prettier than me? I need to know that."

"You won't listen, will you? You won't believe a damn thing I'm saying."

"What is she like?"

"What the hell does it take to convince you?"

"You sat back in the corner in a booth and it was too dark for me to see what she looked like. If I had only started dreaming a minute earlier! When you were outside under the light!"

"You're crazy, you know that? You and your dreams. You're crazy."

"Behind the bar, usually there's a mirror. But not so at At's Place. There's a large picture of a bull and it's in a gold frame. Underneath it says, *Bull Durham*. Am I right?"

"Listen, I've told you before. . .I have never been in At's Place. He might have a bull tied to the bar for all I know."

"Will you take me there? I've got to know."

"No, I sure as hell won't take you there. It's crazy."

"I've got to know."

"All right." He looked at her, his eyes darting around her form on the bed. "All right, I'll take you on one condition."

"I've just got to."

"I'll take you if you promise to quit all this crazy talk about your damned old dreams."

"You'll take me?"

"If you promise."

"I've got to know."

"You'll see. Crazy, that's all. Just plain crazy. A Bull Durham sign!"

"I've got to."

His steel grey eyes were staring at the crack in the ceiling when the light began to come in. Usually he watched dawn from the porch but this morning he lay still and thought of all the little shadows jumping around the trees like rabbits and he thought of darkness buried in the crack, and even when the room had all the light it could hold, the black line on the ceiling stayed.

"You awake?"

He didn't say anything but continued staring at that dark line.

"Joe Jim?"

"Yes, I'm awake."

"I'm sorry."

"Forget it."

"No, I really am."

"I said forget it."

"No, listen. You've got to understand."

"What's to understand?" His eyes claimed the coldness of the dark crack on the ceiling.

"No, listen. It's just I can't. I want to but I can't. Not when I think of her."

"I've told you. There's no one." He turned on his side, away from her.

They stopped just before going onto the blacktop which led to Hindeman. She didn't say anything but stood waiting for him. He looked back the way they came and then along the blacktop toward Hindeman.

"Now you've got to promise. When we get to At's Place and

you find there's no damned old bull sign, you'll forget all this foolishness."

"I know it'll be there." She looked at the ground and then along the blacktop.

"Yes, but if it's not, you've got to promise."

She shook her head yes.

They didn't say anything else and the cars flashing by, whipping the wind up, didn't slow their movement.

As they moved along the street there were sounds of a town coming alive in midmorning and even someone shouting, "Hey, Joe Jim," but he didn't look aside, and the recognition, the call, was drowned in the muffled sound of shoes on the sidewalk.

Then they were there. They stood under the sign hung on an iron bar extending out over the sidewalk, *At's Place* which swung back and forth in an easy shifting wind maybe the beginning signs of a coming afternoon thunderstorm.

"See. It's just like I saw it in my dream. Even the scraping sound."

"You've been past it hundreds of times. You just remembered it, that's all."

"But I've never been inside. That couldn't be something I'm remembering."

"You're not the only one."

They stood inside, not looking at each other, not saying anything, but staring at the bull in the gold frame behind the bar. Below the picture in gold letters were the words, "Bull Durham."

"Something I can do for you?" asked the bartender.

Joe Jim shook his head no.

After they left the blacktop, they stopped.

"I just wish I knew what she looked like."

"I told you, there's no. . ." Then he shook his head but said nothing else.

"I'll be leaving in the morning."

He shook his head yes. He was looking down, rubbing his feet in the scratchy gravel and thinking of a yellow leaf—first whole, then in small broken pieces, then gone.

Elizabeth Madox Roberts

SACRIFICE OF THE MAIDENS

An unnatural dusk lay among the pillars of the little chapel and the candle-glow struggled with the white of the late daylight that came through the windows. Felix Barbour walked along the aisle beside Lester, his brother, and sat in a pew which a nun, who acted as usher, had already pointed out for his sister, Piety. Outside he heard the crying of the crickets and a shrill pulse of frogs that lived about the pond in the field beyond the convent park. Inside were other sounds which were more near and more full of power, the sounds made by a gathering of many people who were hushed to quiet, whose garments whispered softly as limbs were settled, as knees left the prayer-stools, as heads were bowed or lifted. The sounds without and those within mingled continually, but the whispers of a throng of bodies worked free of the cries that came from the outer wet and the grass.

The strangeness of the little chapel, a chapel for the worship of nuns, put a strangeness over his sense of himself as being present, as being a part of the praying throng. The seat seemed small and scarcely sufficient for his large strong limbs as he crumpled himself to rest there, and his bulk seemed awkward on the prayer-stool. That night his sister, Anne, would take the first vows which would make her a nun of the Dominican Order, and he had come now to witness the strange ceremony. He had known in a vague and troubled way that this would be the end of Anne. This knowing dispersed now under the strangeness of the chapel, under the temporary cramping posture of his limbs, as if the old way would be restored when he stretched himself to his stature and walked again into the outer air. Anne had come home from the convent school during the Easter vacation to tell those at home that she would take the vows. Sitting beside the fire, she had risen suddenly, flinging back from the doorway as she stood in the act of going:

"I aim to take the vows, to live the holy life. I aim . . . That's my intention. . . ."

This was followed by a hush that settled over the house broken by their father's awkward protest and then his silent acceptance. Now a warm breath spread over the chapel, the breath of a multitude of men brought together to act as one being. All the congregation had begun to chant the Rosary in recitative, all standing. The priest in the altar would begin, half singing, but on a word, a Word, the congregation would break over him, covering his voice with a rush of acclamation and petition, the whole making a spoken fugue, the many-ply voice of the congregation speaking all together in a rushing chant that ran level with the heads of men and spread laterally beyond, rushing forward. The priest, speaking first then, rapidly intoning:

Hail Mary, full of grace,
Blessed art thou among women
Blessed is the fruit of thy . . .

Over this, over the word, then broke the cries of the people while the priest held the intoned word as a fundamental tone, their words falling swiftly spoken, his word delayed. While he boomed the great thundering word they continued, these words being the whole of their saying:

Holy Mary, Mother of God,
Pray for us now and at the hour of our death . . .

But the priest had begun again, making again the swift words that opened the chant, and the people fell into a stillness that was like dust, a world destroyed. The people were nothing, they had fallen, their cries were lost and they had become the ashes of a burnt-out life, and extinct order. They fell away in a soft patter, not all in one falling, a few surviving one instant beyond the general death, but presently these were lost to the last soul, "hour of our death . . . our death . . ." the last dusty patter, the last expiring utterance. Over this destruction the priest had already begun the onward rush of a new creation:

Hail Mary, full of grace,
Blessed art thou among women
Blessed is the fruit of thy . . .

The great intoned word again, and the people are alive. A great rush of human living and all sprang into life instantly in one act of creation while the immense thundering word under them was a power to push them forward and on. Held again as the fundamental and richly intoned, it survived while they ran forward with their lifetime, their creation, their prayers and cries, their falling away at last into the words of departure.

> Holy Mary, Mother of God,
> Pray for us now and at the hour of our death . . .

Over and over this regeneration and death continued, running around the entire cycle of the Rosary, the Our Father of the large bead partaking of the same pattern, borrowing from the general chant. A mystery stood in a clear pattern, but was not entirely revealed to him, and Felix remembered Anne intently, seeing her from first to last in a sharp sense of her whole being which was made up of pictures and sounds and odors and remembered ways.

He fell into a half dream, his drooping eyes resting on his bent fingers as they lay on his lax thighs. It was a March day three years earlier. The wind was hurling laughter about among the trees and making laughter cry out of the creaking hinge of the barn gate. He walked out to the pasture to salt the young cattle, the yearlings that were feeding there, and as he walked he knew the odors of the salt that came up from the old basket in his hand. The herd came, eager to get what he had brought, and he walked among them, spreading the piles in three places so that all might have a share. The plump calves pushed one another away from the salt, and they bent their greedy muzzles to lick at the stones. While their smooth, sleek coats moved away in the sun and the wind he knew suddenly that there was a loveliness in girls and knew that he had only of late become aware of their prettiness, of their round soft flesh and the shy, veiled laughter that hid under their boldness, even under their profane words when they made as if they were angry, when they enacted distrust and put blame or blight on some matter. They carried a kindness within them that put away any anger that might leap out of their tongues. Walking back toward the house he met Anne in the path.

"What way did the turkey hen go?" she asked him.

He saw that she had grown into a prettiness, that she had put on all that he had been dreaming. A gentleness had come into her body. She had become precious to all men as she stood in the path. His voice was answering her, teasing, "The turkey hens are a woman's work."

"God's own sake, you are a mean boy, Felix Barbour. Won't tell whe'r you saw the old hen or not!"

He heard her calling the turkeys from the distant fence where the pasture gave way to the new field of wheat. Standing on the rail of the fence she was a child again, Annie, scarcely anything at all. She was a thin childish crying that called home the straying fowls.

The great wheel of the Rosary was running forward, rolling over men as they stood in the attitudes of prayer, the priest saying the swift chant:

Hail Mary, full of grace,
Blessed art thou among women
Blessed is the fruit . . .

Summer and winter and Anne, they were running down the channel of the year. The year spread widely then, as if it flowed abroad to fill a wide field with corn. There was sweetness in the high blades of the corn and abundance in the full shucks as he tore each ear from the ripe stem.

"What price will it bring?" Anne was asking. She was standing beside the shock, her basket filled with corn for the turkeys. The half-green corn was hard to break from the ear, and her hands were burnt and sore from the tough husks. "What price will corn bring?" she was asking.

Felix named three other girls quickly, calling three names in his memory while Anne stood beside the shock to ask of the corn. There was a newer prettiness in her laugh and a fresh way of being a woman in her bent cheek when she smiled. He told the value of the corn and the measure of it in bushels to the acre. A four-ply measure of a woman's loveliness passed then down the rows of the cut field and went toward the pen where the turkeys were kept in autumn, and Felix smiled inwardly as he bent to tear apart the shock to get the inner ears. His thought floated on his floating breath where it came and went in his chest, where it beat a rhythm of nothingness against his throat. The picture of the autumn corn faded and the dry odors of the blades of fodder gave way before the crying of the frogs in the wet grass, but these fell away with the pattering death cries of supplicating men and the greater voice boomed and droned the new creation:

Hail Mary, full of grace,
Blessed art thou among women . . .

The thunder broke on the word and the rattle of voices rushed from the sons of men who burst again into being. The first cries of the priest leaped over his thought of Anne and the three girls he had named. He saw Anne playing with the dog in the yard, saw her running after a chicken to drive it into a coop, saw her making herself a dress to wear to the convent school. She was talking to Dominic Brady beside the gate. She was gone from home, she was remembered clearly, remembered vaguely, forgotten, remembered, she was here, gone, everywhere present. She was saying that she would take the vows, standing beside the door to say this, making a departure to fit her words. A creation had been destroyed; it was falling away now into a clatter of weary death in the hurried leavings of old sayings that dropped from the mouths of weary men. But the priest had opened the earth anew and brought out a new dark vigor of life. There were remembered ways of girls in his leaping words of creation. They were soft to touch, they were given to laughter, easy to come to tears, easy with pity, easy with anger. They easily became women. His thought waked again from its repose on his folded hands. The chant of the Rosary was suddenly finished. The people seated themselves with a broken patter of infinite whispers made by shifting bodies and the ending postures of prayer.

The organ in the loft at the rear of the chapel began to play the Mendelssohn wedding march. It was played, not passionately, as in a human wedding, but softly, legato, as if it were played in a dream. Then Felix knew that the persons of the procession were coming, that they were walking into the chapel. Their coming was like the coming of the doves, was a soft moving of wings. Looking backward quickly he saw that two nuns walked before carrying lighted tapers. The four postulants came then in the procession, walking two and two, and behind them came two novices carrying tapers. The lights from the candles fell on the faces of the women who carried them and lit up the inner surfaces of their white cowls and made more beautiful the life in their cheeks and their brows. The postulants were dressed as brides, each one wearing a white dress and a long white veil that was fastened with a wreath about the hair. They walked, two together, their hands folded as supplicants. A dark-haired girl and a full-breasted girl walked first. Then Anne and her companion, who was a tall slender girl, came. All stepped slowly, their little white shoes making no noise on the smooth boards of the aisle floor.

When their shadows passed him Felix glanced toward Lester, his brother, to see how this passing had touched him. The boy was sitting very still, his hands steady, his thought as if it slept on his folded hands. Their sister, Piety, was married. She had been married out of their home for a number of years and she seemed, therefore, as someone who was related to them, not as one of them. She seemed to be kinsfolk. Felix looked at her intently to see what surrounded her now in this strange moment while Anne mounted the aisle and went toward the altar steps. Three children drifted in the air about Piety, all of them dead now, all hers. She was watching Anne mount the steps in a happy rapture, looking out from behind the fog of the children.

Anne was very small as she stood beside the tall girl whose wreath filled with a fine grace over her brown hair. The girls were kneeling in the altar now, bowing over their supplicating hands, and as they bowed the tall girl's rounded cheek showed beyond the line of her shoulder. The priest before the altar had a care never to turn his back upon the holies there, but if he had need to cross from one side to the other he turned about and faced whatever was there housed. While he talked of the solemnity of the hour and the sacredness of the rites enacted, his words flattened to a stillness and Felix watched Anne and the girl who wore the wreath with singular grace. She sat or knelt beside Anne, and the two together made a loveliness that surrounded their being and gave a softly shed presence that reached his senses even when he looked away from them, which came home to him with a new pleasure and satisfaction when he returned his look to the place where they waited.

The choir above began to chant a thin hymn to God, a faint, high-pitched, unsonorous singing of nuns and girls, making beautiful Latin vows over the seated multitude. The hour delayed and fell drowsily apart. Felix knew, in the interval that grew into the severed hour, what manner of smile would come to the tall girl's face and how her thin lips would part to speak and how her head would bow over prayers or work. He knew how her eyes would follow printed words over a page or how she would walk out into the sunlight and what her tall lithe flesh would be as it passed over a farm, as it went within doors. He wondered what name he should call her by in his mind and a vapor of fine names poured over his thought. He loved his sister Anne entirely then and was pleased that she knelt near the tall lovely girl whom he named now with these remote pleasures. These two, dressed as brides, in their white lace and thin veils, knelt together a little apart from the other two brides who knelt at the right of the altar, and in his thought he once slipped quietly between the two, Anne and the named one whom he could not name, and took each by the arm to cherish both forever, but this vague wish died slowly in the mind as if some inner hand forbade it, but his eyes clung then to the bent head of the tall girl and saw again the pink of her cheek and the line of her shoulder.

The priest was giving the brides then the garments they were to wear, piece by piece. The tunic was laid first on their outstretched hands. It was folded neatly together and was made of some soft white wool cloth, and the priest called it by its symbolic name, naming it with a speech. When he had given the tunic he turned to the table at his left where other garments were folded. The tall girl took her garments onto her extended hands with an exquisite care. Felix dwelt rather with her bowed head, her faintly tinted cheek, with the fall of her veil and the droop of her wreath, with the line of her throat beneath her veil and the round curve of her shoulder. The priest gave them the girdle or cincture, placing each coiled in a ring upon the folds of the tunic as each girl held it on her flattened hands, and he named its significance with solemn words. The pile of things on the table beside the altar was diminishing and the ceremony rolled along, the hour severed now and lost out of its nearness, touching Felix as a ceremony that went from him remotely as did recurring prayers, while he longed to know the girl's exact name and be able to say it in his mind, to name his sense of her loveliness with a word.

The priest was giving the scapular, the most essential part of the habit, he said, the gift of the Virgin. All the last burdens were laid now, one by one, upon the outstretched palms of the girls, for he had given the veil, symbol he said of modesty.

"It will cover you," he said.

It would be the symbol of their poverty, chastity, and obedience. The wedding march was played again and the girls came from the altar, led by the two novices with the lighted tapers.

Each girl carried her precious burdens on her outstretched palms, as she had taken them, and each looked forward, seeing neither the right nor the left, as she passed. Their small steps were set down softly on the bars of the faintly played march and they went out of the chapel into some hidden part of the convent.

The choir chanted again, another high thin hymn, the singing of girls, and Felix heard girls laughing through the thin outcry of the chant, heard remembered laughter blowing in a wind through the settled bars of the incantation. He heard Anne running down the yard at their farm to drive a hen away from the little turkeys while they had their food under the lilac bush, and he heard her shout in the wind and heard her laugh when the old hen flew wildly over a fence to escape her clamor. Again he wanted the name of the tall fair girl and he felt the touch of soft light hands at his brow and at his throat, the hands of the tall girl fluttering over his face and touching his shoulder, and he felt himself open as if to give out some fine inner essence of himself. He lived upon the laughter that flowed under the hymn and lived swiftly as haunted by an unrealized disaster that threatened to arise from some hidden part and bring the whole earth to a swift consummation. Opened to give all that he had in the brief moments left to life, he thought more minutely of the fair girl's graceful splendors of being and he knew entirely what her laughter would be, longing then for her name, for some word that would signify herself and name his own delight in her.

The steps came back to the tread of the hymn which the voices in the loft had rounded to an amen. The girls wore now the long white robes of young nuns and on their heads were the stiff veils of the women of the holy order. As they passed, Felix looked up into their faces and saw them, recognizing each one with a pleasure in the recognition. The tall girl wore her linen veil as he knew she would and carried her scapular with her own grace, as if she loaned her grace temporarily to it. The priest met them in the sanctuary and again they were kneeling. The priest was giving them their last gifts. He was giving them their rosaries, the long pattern by which, as nuns, they would pray. Then he was giving them their names.

Felix felt a leaping within his heart to know that he would now hear the name of the lovely girl called and would know it thereafter. The priest was speaking, the large girl at the right of the altar knelt before him:

"You were known in the world as Annette Stevenson."

There was a pause, and Felix flung far across the country to a house on Severn Creek, the home of the Stevensons. His mind was leaping swiftly with recognition and expectations. But the priest was speaking again, taking back all that he had given:

"Your name henceforth will be Sister Mary Agnes."

He had turned from the large girl now to her companion and what passed there went over in a dull dream, a name given and taken away. The priest now turned his back to the congregation and passed the holies, going toward the left of the altar, toward the two small figures that knelt there. A pleasure leaped up within Felix to know that he would now know the name of the lovely girl and he leaped forward in mind to take the name, his thought already caressing it.

The voice leaned above the slender figure that knelt next and said:

"In the world you were known as Aurelia Bannon . . ."

Aurelia, then. He had it. A dim sense of consummation and satisfaction played over him. He stirred in his place and shifted his hands, gratified. Aurelia was the name. He might have known, he reflected, that this lovely creature would carry such a name. It filled his entire mind and flowed over into his sense of all that he had seen of her. But the priest was speaking, continuing, making solemn words over the leaning girl, and Felix caught again at what he had said and held it to try to stay what would follow, but this was useless. The voice moved forward, having spoken the first pronouncement:

"You were known in the world as Aurelia Bannon . . .

"Henceforth your name will be Sister Mary Dolores."

The world broke and disaster followed. The ashes of a burnt-out creation rattled and pattered down the endless cliffs of shales and Felix was aware of the rasping breath in his throat, was aware of Anne, of the last of the kneeling postulants, the smallest figure. She knelt bowed, as if to take the pronouncement on her bent shoulders. The priest had soon finished. He moved slightly and settled over the small kneeler, saying softly, as if he were already done:

"In the world you were known as Anne Barbour . . .

"Henceforth your name will be Sister Magdalen."

James Still

MRS. RAZOR

"We'll have to do something about that child," Father said. We sat in the kichen, eating our supper, though day still held and the chickens had not yet gone to roost in the gilly trees. Elvy was crying behind the stove, and her throat was raw with sobbing. Morg and I paused, bread in hand, and glanced over our shoulders. The firebox of the Cincinnati stove winked, the iron flowers of the oven throbbed with heat. Mother tipped a finger to her lips, motioning Father to hush. Father's voice lifted:—

"I figure a small thrashing would make her leave off this foolish notion."

Elvy was six years old. She was married, to hear her tell it, and had three children and a lazy shuck of a husband who cared not a mite for his own and left his family to live upon her kin. The thought had grown into truth in her mind. I could play at being Brother Hemp Leckett, climb onto a chopblock and preach to the fowls; or I could be Round George Harks, riding the creeks, killing all who crossed my path; I could be any man body. Morg couldn't make-believe; he was just Morg. But Elvy had imagined herself old and thrown away by a husband, and she kept believing.

"A day will come," Elvy told us, "when my man's going to get killed down dead, the way he's living." She spoke hard of her husband and was a shrew of a wife who thought only of her children; she was as busy with her young as a hen with biddies. It was a dog's life she led, washing rags of clothes, sewing with a straw for needle, singing by the half hour to cradled arms, and keeping an eye sharp for gypsies. She jerked at loose garments and fastened and pinned, as Mother did to us.

Once we spied her in the grape arbor making to put a jacket on a baby that wouldn't hold still. She slapped the air, saying, "Hold up, young'un!" Morg stared, half believing. Later she claimed her children were stolen. It wasn't by the dark people. Her husband had taken them—she didn't know where. For days she sat pale and small, minced her victuals, and fretted in her sleep. She had wept, "My man's the meanest critter ever was. Old Scratch is bound to get him."

And now Elvy's husband was dead. She had run to Mother to tell this thing, the news having come in an unknown way. She waited dry-eyed and shocked until Father rode in from the fields in middle afternoon and she met him at the barn gate to choke out her loss.

"We've got to haste to Biggety Creek and fetch my chaps ere the gypsies come," she grieved. "They're left alone."

"Doornail dead?" Father had asked, smiling to hear Biggety Creek named, the Nowhere Place he had told us of once at table. Biggety Creek where heads are the size of water buckets, where noses are turned up like old shoes, women wear skillets for hats, and men screw their breeches on, and where people are so proper they eat with little fingers pointing, and one pea at a time. Father rarely missed a chance to preach us a sermon.

"We've got to haste," Elvy pled.

"Do you know the road to Biggety Creek?"

Elvy nodded.

Father keened his eyes to see what manner of chap was his own, his face lengthening and his patience wearing thin. He grabbed his hat off and clapped it angrily against his leg; he strode into the barn, fed the mules, and came to the house with Elvy tagging after and weeping.

"Fix an early supper," he told Mother.

Father's jaws were set as he drew his chair to the table. The day was still so bright the wall bore a shadow of the unkindled lamp. Elvy had hidden behind the stove, lying on the cat's pallet, crying. "Come and eat your victuals," Mother begged, for her idea was to humor children and let them grow out of their notions. But Elvy would not.

II

We knew Father's hand itched for a hickory switch. Disobedience angered him quicker than anything. Yet he only looked worried. The summer long he had teased Elvy, trying to shake her belief. Once while shaving he had asked, "What ever made you marry that lump of a husband, won't come home, never furnishes a cent?" Morg and I stood by to spread the leftover lather on our faces and scrape it off with a kitchen knife. "I say it's past strange I've not met my own son-in-law.

I hunger to shake his hand and welcome him to the family, ask him to sit down to our board and stick his feet under."

Father had glanced slyly at Elvy. "What's his name? Upon my honor I haven't been told."

Elvy looked up. Her eyes glassed in thought. "He's called Razor."

"Given name or family?"

"Just Razor."

"Ask him to come," Father urged in mock seriousness. "Invite him up for Sunday dinner."

Elvy had promised that her husband would come. She had Mother fry a chicken, the dish he liked best, claiming the gizzard was his chosen morsel. Nothing less than the flax tablecloth was good enough, and she gathered spiderwort blossoms for the centerpiece. An extra chair was placed, and we waited; we waited noon through, until one o'clock. Then she told us confidentially, "Go ahead and eat. Razor allus was slow as Jim Christmas." She carried a bowl of soup behind the Cincinnati stove to feed her children. In the evening she explained, "I've learnt why my man stayed away. He hain't got a red cent to his pocket and he's scared o' being lawed for not supporting his chaps."

Father had replied, "I need help—need a workhand to grub corn ground. A dollar a day I'll pay, greenback on the barrel top. I want a feller with lard in his elbows and willing to work. Fighting sourwood sprouts is like going to war. If Razor has got the measure of the job, I'll hire him and promise not to law."

"I ought never to a-took him for a husband," Elvy confessed. "When first I married he was smart as ants. Now he's turned so lazy he won't even fasten his gallus buckles. He's slouchy and no 'count."

"Humm," Father had grunted, eying Morg and me, the way our clothes hung on us. "Sloth works on a feller," he preached. "It grows roots. He'll start letting his sleeves flare and shirttail go hang. One day he gets too sorry to bend and lace his shoes, and it's a *swarp*, *swarp* every step. A time comes he'll not latch the top button of his breeches—ah, when a man turns his potty out, he's beyond cure."

"That's Razor all over," Elvy had said.

Father's teasing had done no good. As we sat at supper that late afternoon, listening to Elvy sob behind the stove, Morg began to stare into his plate and could eat no more. He believed Elvy. Tears hung on his chin.

Father's face tightened, half in anger, half in dismay. He lifted his hands in defeat. "Hell's bangers!" he blurted.

I whispered to Morg, "Razor is a lie-tale." Morg's tears fell thicker. I spoke small into his ear, "Act it's not so," but Morg could never make-like.

Father suddenly thrust back his chair. "Hurry and get ready," he ordered, "the whole push of you. We're going to Biggety Creek." His voice was as dry as a stick.

Elvy's sobbing hushed. Morg blinked. The room became so quiet I could hear flames eating wood in the firebox. Father arose and made long-legged strides toward the barn to harness the mules.

We mounted the wagon, Father and Mother to the spring seat, Elvy settling between; I stood with Morg behind the seat. Dusk was creeping out of the hollows. Chickens walked toward the gilly trees, flew to their roosts, sleepy and quarrelsome. Father gathered the reins and angled the whip to start the mules. "Now, which way?" he asked Elvy. She pointed ahead and we rode off.

The light faded. Night came. The shapes of trees and fences were lost and there were only the wise eyes of the mules to pick the road when the ground had melted and the sky was gone. Elvy nodded fitfully, trying to keep awake. We traveled six miles before Father turned back.

Jane Stuart

TULLIE

"Joy to the world, Miss Savage, Joy to the world, Mommy's had a little boy, and I have a brother. Joy to the world, Miss Savage, Jesus has sent us a son and I won't be lonely no more." Tullie ran skipping through the field of daisies and dandelions, running her bare thin feet across the cold spring grass and making her toes wriggle each blade she could catch between them.

"Joy, joy, Miss Savage. Daddy's coming home to see my brother Ed. Maybe he'll be so happy now that he will stay with us. Maybe we're going to be a storybook family after all."

Tullie ran up and down the field, zigzagging her way through the neat rows of flowers that the wind had sewn in the green spring meadow. Her bare feet ran skipping, her cold legs hurried behind them, faster and faster, hurrying to keep up with the narrow feet that slid and skipped across the early March grass.

On my way from Easter Gap,
On my way to see my pap,
Going home to my brother Ed,
Fast asleep in my mommy's bed.

Tullie sang and danced in the meadow until, tired, she flopped down beside the brown fallen tree that lay across a dry creekbed and marked, in Tullie's mind, the boundaries between her meadow and the land that lay beyond.

She lay on her back, her face turned up to the sky, counting kittens and dogs that tumbled by in the white somersaulting clouds. Oh wonder day, she thought, when the little boy Jesus put the kitten and dogs that have died on earth up in the clouds. Now I can watch them go by, and I can be happy because I know that they are.

"No, he's not, no he's not, brown baron," she said suddenly to the wind in passing. "My little dog's not drowned and lying in the bottom of the Sandy River. My daddy didn't drown my dog and drop him there. My doggie ran away, the night before Christmas, and the little boy Jesus found him and put him in the clouds. He's up there now, chasing cats and looking for me." Tullie lay on the cold ground and watched the sky, her fingers grabbing for acorns and prodding them into the still hard ground.

Then she heard the school bell ringing. Far away, the bell was ringing to tell her that she must hurry, or she would be late again. Late to school, late to Miss Savage's classroom, late to the boys and girls who stared at her and frightened her and made her lose her voice and forget what she had to say. Late to watch them looking at her, laughing at her, making fun of her behind her back, or sometimes, when Miss Savage wasn't watching, to her face.

"Lord, Lord, I have to run," she said. She leaped from the ground and began her zigzag dance across the dry creekbed, leaving her meadow, crossing to the land that lay beyond.

Down the hill she went, fast as the wind, brown-baron wind that was following her, puffing, hurrying to keep up with her slim feet and long lean legs. Laughing and crying to herself at once, as she thought about Mommy at home in bed with her new brother Ed, her secret, her own secret come true. Laughing and crying as she thought about Daddy over in Carson, sure to hear the news and come home to see them all.

It's not Christmas now, Daddy, you don't have to bring us no presents, she thought. Just come and see us. Just come.

As she neared the slope of the hill, she stopped running and began to walk. Her walk was slow, her right foot twisted in the grass and fell limp, dragging itself along behind her left foot. In her mind, she could hear them already, saying to each other, "Here comes Tullie, late and lame! Tullie, Tullie, that's her name!" She tried to stand tall but her shoulders began to crimp, and she could not pull herself up straight. So she walked slowly, hunched forward, the right foot twisting itself behind the left that struggled to make a way through the stubbled grass.

"Come recess today and I am going to play," she said, as she neared the school. "I am going to play Red Rover and I am going to run so hard and throw myself at them with all my strength. I'll break Priscilla's arm, I'll hit her so hard. I'll make her scream. Then she won't say nothing to me again."

Miss Savage said, as she came in the room, "You're late again, Tullie."

Tullie bowed her head, said nothing, and slipped into her seat in the back row.

"Do you want lunch?"

Tullie kept her head down low, and nodded only once. It was her sign to Miss Savage. Miss Savage knew the sign, and she made a checkmark by Tullie's name on the lunch list.

"You've got to pay," the boy in front of her said, under his breath.

"I've got no money," Tullie snapped.

"See, Miss Savage, she can talk," Bill Bowen said. "She can talk, I heard her."

"That will be enough, Bill," Miss Savage said. She went to the blackboard and continued writing out arithmetic problems. "Copy these on your papers, and begin to work them," she said, her back still to the class.

Priscilla Mayhew turned around from her seat in the front row and stuck out her tongue at Tullie.

"Stop it, stop it, stop it," Tullie said under her breath. "I'll break your arm if you don't."

She made a face back, turning her mouth down at the corners and crossing her eyes at Priscilla.

"Ooh, Miss Savage," Priscilla screamed, jumping up as if Bill Bowen had left a tack on her seat. "She put a hex on me. I saw her."

Miss Savage faced the class. "Priscilla, what are you talking about?"

"Tullie Cameron. I saw her do it. She's putting a hex on me. She's got the devil's eye, and she's making it work on me."

"Priscilla!" Miss Savage said. "That will be enough."

"But Miss Savage . . ."

"Priscilla, one more word from you and I am going to take you to the principal's office. Now sit facing the blackboard and do your arithmetic."

Priscilla took up her pencil and began to copy down the addition and subtraction. But she couldn't concentrate. She felt Tullie's hex crawling up and down her neck, she felt the devil's eye sneaking under the collar of her dress. Her mind wouldn't work. She couldn't add, she couldn't subtract. She couldn't hold the pencil upright, and the paper kept slipping out from under her hand.

In the back seat, Tullie held the tip of her own pencil on her tongue and stared at the board, trying to make out what the numbers were.

Bill Bowen moved aside so that Tullie could copy from his paper.

"You did very well today, Tullie," Miss Savage said, when she came around to check their answers. "You have been studying, haven't you?"

Tullie ducked her head down between her shoulders and grinned into the wood of the desk.

Then there was a knock on the door and Pam Braden who sat in the chair by the door today because it was her turn to answer it, jumped up and almost stumbled across her feet in her hurry to yank the door open.

"Principal's office," said a big eighth grader.

"Miss Savage," Pam squeaked, "Miss Savage."

Miss Savage came to the door. "Yes?" And she took the note from the big eighth grader's hand that was stretched out like an evil paw to hand over its evil message.

"Straight from the devil," Tullie thought.

Miss Savage sighed. "Tullie, could I speak to you in the hall?" she said.

Tullie pulled herself out of her seat, slowly, the second time Miss Savage spoke to her, and limped toward the door.

"I told you you were going to get it," Priscilla hissed as she went out.

As she pulled the door shut, Tullie grinned wildly at Priscilla Mayhew, showing the inside of her mouth, half empty of teeth, full of pink swollen gums.

"Ooh," Priscilla said. "She's done it again."

The class tittered.

"Tullie," Miss Savage said, when the door was shut and there was no one else in the hall. "Tullie," and the hall was quiet and black, no lights, no sounds of feet shuffling or children coughing as they opened and closed their books. "I have a note from the principal's office. You went down to the third grade yesterday afternoon, didn't you?"

She said nothing.

"Didn't you, Tullie? Don't you remember? I said you could go, in the afternoon, to sit with the little ones and listen to the stories."

"Yes, yes, yes, I went."

Miss Savage sighed. "Tullie, Miss Longer says her watch is missing and that some of the children say you took it. Is that true?"

The hall was black and quiet, silent, dark, no voices, no joy, no little boy Jesus sitting there to watch. And listen.

No, no, Miss Savage, you know I wouldn't do nothing like that, she said to herself. You know I'm not that kind of person. I'm a good girl, Miss Savage, I'm good and they say awful things about me because they don't like me and they tell their kids not to have anything to do with me. So they say awful things about me and try to hurt me so I'll go away and never come back.

"Tullie, are you listening?"

Tullie nodded.

"Tullie, do you know anything about the watch?"

"No."

"All right. Shall we go down and talk with Miss Longer?"

I don't want to go there. I don't want to go down there and have them all laughing at me. They don't like me. They took the watch and put it in my shoe. When I wasn't looking. They put it there, when one of them was sitting on my lap and the other had her hands over my eyes and another one was holding my arms behind me. I couldn't help it. But I didn't take the watch. I'm not that kind of person.

"Shall we go, Tullie?"

"No."

"Then will you go and get the watch?"

Tullie limped back inside the room, back to her desk in the end row. She leaned down and looked into the black hole of her desk, she stuck her hand into the big square beehive and prodded among the books and wads of storybook paper. Then she squatted on the floor and reached again, working her fingers through the paper until she came upon the little wad that held the watch. She took out the watch, wrapped in a square of red construction paper, folded neatly, and stuck it into her arithmetic book.

"Tullie's going to be in a match," Bill Bowen whispered, and everyone laughed.

She hurried back to the door, her face on fire, limping as fast as she could go, her heart thumping under the thin cotton of her dress. "Here," she said, and stuck the book at Miss Savage. "Here, take it."

Miss Savage opened the book and took out the watch. It was still running.

"Why did you take it?"

"Didn't take it."

"I'll have to talk to the principal, Tullie."

Tullie bowed her head.

"Do you want to wait for me inside, or come along?"

Tullie hurried back to her seat, folded her arms on her desk, put down her head, and cried. No one in the room said anything. Her classmates sat very still, very quiet, listening to Tullie's sobs. Pam Braden sat up tall in her chair, pencil and tablet on her desk. She was to take the names of anyone who talked while Miss Savage was out of the room.

"Don't cry, Tullie," Bill Bowen whispered, looking straight ahead of him so that Pam Braden wouldn't be able to see him turned around, and catch him talking. "Don't cry."

Tullie sobbed louder. Her classmates shuffled their feet under their desks and opened and closed their books. Then Priscilla Mayhew got out of her seat and walked back to the back of the room, with a book to put in her locker. She stopped behind Tullie's desk and put her hand on Tullie's shoulder. "Don't cry, Tullie," she whispered. "It'll be all right. I know it will. Please don't cry. We won't tease you any more."

"Ooh," Tullie cried aloud.

"You can play with us at recess." It was all that Priscilla could say.

It was everything that Tullie wanted. She stopped her crying, wiped her red swollen eyes with an arm, and smiled at Priscilla. Seeing her smile that way, with her mouth open, frightened Priscilla, who remembered what her mother had said about not talking to Tullie or she might catch whatever it was that Tullie had.

Miss Savage came back into the room and erased the board. It was time for spelling. They began to copy their spelling words onto their lined tablet paper, and the bell rang.

"First row line up," Pam Braden said.

The first row scrambled to its feet and formed a straight line at the door.

"Second row," Pam Braden called. "Third, fourth, and fifth rows."

Then Miss Savage opened the door and the long neat line went quietly down the hall, breaking as the big door was opened and boys and girls spilled out into the yard, heading for swings, slides, baseball, and a big empty field where a game of Red

Rover was already being started by the fifth graders who fled when they saw the sixth grade thundering out behind Priscilla Mayhew.

The third time around, somebody called Red Rover, Red Rover, send Tullie right over.

Tullie grinned and hid her face behind her arm.

"Go on, Tullie," Jo Ann Jackson said. "Go on."

"Can't."

"Don't push her, Jo Ann," William Sizemore said. "You know she can't run."

Yes I can run, I can run, I can run, Tullie thought. And, flapping her arms like the wings of a big bird, she began to jump up and down to gather speed. When she was going strong, Jo Ann gave her a push and she began to hurdle across the field, toward the line that had moved in a little so she wouldn't have so far to go.

Here I come, here I come, I'm a bird and I can fly, Tullie sang to herself.

She threw herself hard at Priscilla Mayhew, but Priscilla saw her coming, screamed, and dropped her arms. On Tullie went, limping and leaping, crashing through space until she stumbled and fell into the dirt at the feet of an eighth grader who was playing outfielder for the big boys.

"Ooh," Tullie cried, and she held her skinned leg in her arms. Miss Savage came running across the field. "Are you all right, Tullie?"

"Ooh," Tullie cried, dazed, looking at the blood trickling down her leg.

"Come with me, I'll get you to first aid." She helped Tullie up and led her across the baseball diamond toward the classrooms.

"What's the trouble?" said Miss Longer, who was on hall duty and ran the first-aid station that week.

"I'm afraid Tullie fell," Miss Savage said. "She was playing Red Rover."

"It's a rough game," Miss Longer said. "Maybe it's too rough for you, Tullie. You ought to be a little more careful." She washed off Tullie's leg, put on some Merthiolate, and a bandage. "You be more careful now, Tullie," she said. "You're not as strong as the others, you know."

Miss Savage helped Tullie back to her homeroom. Her leg was hurting and she wanted to sit down at her desk and put her white face in her arms.

"You see, Tullie," Miss Savage said, "you needn't have been afraid of Miss Longer. She likes you. She told me not to go to the principal about her watch. She said that she knows you and she is sure that it won't happen again."

That isn't true, Miss Savage, Tullie thought. I know you went to the principal, and I know he told you not to bother, that I'm too dumb to understand. I've heard him talking about me before. They all think I'm too dumb to understand. They think I'm dumb, and stupid, and crazy. They think I'm a witch because their mothers tell them my mommy is a witch.

Thinking of her mother again, Tullie began to rock back and forth in the seat, holding her hurt leg close to her. "Joy, joy," she whispered, "Joy, I've got a baby brother. When I go home today I will see my baby brother Ed. Joy to the world, my mommy will hold him up for me to see and let me play with him. Then tonight maybe my daddy will come home and we can be together, all of us together, just like a storybook family."

At the lunch hour, she sat with her back to Miss Savage and heard the other teachers talking. "I guess it's true," Mrs. Hicks was saying. "I guess there is another baby."

"Whose this time?"

"I don't know. There's a man living there now."

"What about Tullie's father?"

"No one's seen him for years."

"Is he still alive?"

"Oh yes. He has a job in the steel mills in Carson. Sends them money from time to time. When he remembers, that is."

"Do you think this will bring him back?"

"Let's hope not. He's no good. The last time he was here. . . . Well, Tullie was really in bad shape for a long time after that."

"What do you mean? Oh, be careful, I think she's listening."

"All right, I'll tell you later."

It wasn't true, any of it. Why did they say those things about her and her mommy? Why did Mrs. Hicks and Miss Madigan say those things about her dad? Evil things, and none of them were true. He didn't hit her, he didn't drown her dog. And her mommy was good and kind, a Disciple of Christ. Joy, joy, joy to the world, they should say. A baby boy, a brother for Tullie. Jesus has sent a little boy. Joy to the world.

"No, go ahead, she can't hear. Poor thing. She can barely see now. We have to take her in to have her eyes examined. And her teeth. . .I'm really worried about her."

"The school doctor will be coming next week. He can examine her. I know that she needs special shoes."

"But who will pay for them?"

"Aren't they on welfare?"

"They can hardly make ends meet, even with that. They'll be no money for glasses or shoes or vitamins. No money for clothes."

"What will she do?"

"Come on, now, Mary. You know these kids better than that. She won't do anything. What can she do? She's poor. Every cent that that mother has will have to go for the baby now."

Miss Savage shook her head. "It's not right," she said. "It just isn't right."

"It may not be right, but that's the way it is."

"I'll help."

"You can't. They wouldn't let you. They've got pride."

"Pride? What's pride when the child is sick and needs medical attention? When she's hungry and needs proper food?"

"Stay out of it, Mary," Mr. Jenkins said. "You'll get the whole family on your head. They can manage. They have so far. You'll see. Someway or other, they'll manage."

Mary Savage left the lunchroom.

Tullie followed her in her mind's eye. Don't take on so, Miss Savage, she thought to herself. Things are all right. You see, I'm not lonely any more. I've got my lunch here, and a baby brother to play with as soon as I get home. Joy to the world!

In the afternoon, the class was tired and quiet and no one said much. Miss Savage read them a story and then they put their heads down on their desks and went to sleep, or worked quietly in their geography workbooks.

Then the bell rang, school was over, and, waving the schoolbus away, Tullie limped off toward the hill that took her up the creekbed home. As she rounded the slope and could no longer see Yellowhawk behind her, she felt free and happy. Her twisted foot uncurled, her slumped shoulders straightened out. Her arms no longer flailed against the wind like huge bird wings pulling her along. She ran gracefully, happily, on fast strong feet to the dandelions and daisies that quilted the green spring meadow with brightness.

On my way home to Easter Gap,
On my way to see my pap,
Going home to my brother Ed,
Fast asleep in my mommy's bed.

When she came to the brown fallen tree that lay stretched across the dry creekbed, she danced over, whirling herself around and around, a zigzagging dervish pushed and pulled by the brown baron wind. She danced and leaped, full of joy, leaving the land that lay beyond behind her. Back in her own meadow, back to her own home.

"Joy to the world, joy, joy, joy to the world, Miss Savage," she sang. "Jesus looks after his own."

Jesse Stuart

WORD AND THE FLESH

Groan leads the way along the cow path; his disciples follow. The cow path is narrow, the pawpaw bushes are clustered on both sides of the path and they are wet with dew. Brother Sluss pulls a pawpaw leaf and licks off the sweet dew with his tongue. Brother Sluss is like a honeybee. The moon floats in the sky like a yellow pumpkin, dark yellowish like the inside of a pumpkin.

Groan and his disciples—Brothers Sluss, Frazier, Shinliver, Littlejohn, Redfern and Pigg—are headed for the Kale Nelson Graveyard. It is approximately one mile away, across Phil Hogan's cow pasture, Ben Lowden's pig lot, Cy Penix's corn patch, thence through the Veil Abraham's peach orchard to a flat where the ribs of an old house (the old Abraham's house) are bleached by the autumn sun and cooled by the autumn night wind. The robe Groan wears is similar to the robe Sunday-school cards picture Christ wearin when He walked and talked with His disciples. It has a low neck, loose flowin sleeves. It is long and tied with a sash at the waist line. The loose sleeves catch on the pawpaw twigs along the path.

"Tell me more about the ten virgins, Brother Groan."

"I don't know about the ten virgins and I ain't discussin the ten virgins. You know there was ten of them, don't you? And you know one of them was Virgin Mary, don't you?"

"Yes, I know that, Brother Groan. But tell me more about them."

"Brother Sluss, we have other things to talk about. Leave me be, won't you? I want to talk with God. I want to feel the sperit. I want to show you what Faith will do tonight. Leave me alone. I am talkin to God now. I am in God's presence. Leave me be, will you?" Brother Groan carries a bundle under one arm. He carries a walkin staff in one hand. His loose sleeves are hard to get between the pawpaw twigs alongside the path.

There is silence. Brother Groan talks to God. They keep movin. They come to the drawbars. One by one they slip between the drawbars, all but Brother Frazier. He is too thick to slip between the rails. He crawls under the bottom rail. Now they are goin through Ben Lowden's pig lot. The moon above them is pretty in the sky. It is still a yellow pumpkin moon—that darkish yellow, the color of the insides of a ripe sun-cooked cornfield pumpkin. The dew on the crab grass in the pig lot sparkles in the yellow moonlight. The September wind slightly rustles the halfway dead pawpaw bushes. The crickets sing, the katydids sing, the whippoorwills quirt-quirt and the owl who-whoos. Brother Groan mutters—an Unknown Tongue whispers to God.

"Brother Groan is goin to show us the Faith tonight."

"Brother Groan is talkin to God."

"No. That is the wind over there in Cy Penix's ripe corn. That is the wind in the corn blades talkin. That is not Sweet Jesus talkin."

"Be quiet, won't you? Brother Groan is tryin to talk to God."

"I ain't said nothin."

"No."

"It is the wind in the fodder blades, I tell you."

"The wind!"

"Didn't I say the wind?"

"Yes, you said the wind."

"Then why did you ask?"

"Because I thought that you said that Brother Sluss said that God whispered."

Brother Groan is first to mount the rail fence. His sleeve catches on one of the stakes-and-riders, but he gets over into Cy Penix's cornfield first. One by one his disciples climb over the fence. Here is the ripe uncut corn in the yellowish wine-colored moonlight. The dead blades are whisperin somethin. Maybe it is: "The dead lie buried here, the dead of ever-so-long-ago. But they lie buried here under the dead roots of this ripe corn."

The corn blades whisper to the wind. There is a sweet dew on these corn blades for Brother Sluss to lick off with his tongue. This dead fodder is buff-colored in the yellowish pumpkin-colored moonlight. Brother Groan leads his disciples through the field of dead corn. There is a ghostly chill of night piercin the thin robe of Brother Groan, and the overalls and the unbuttoned shirts of his disciples.

There is a loneliness in the night, in the moonlight that covers the land and in the wind among the trees. There is something lonely about dead leaves rakin against one's clothes at night, for they too seem to say: "The dead lie buried here, the dead of ever-so-long-ago. But they lie buried here under the livin roots of these autumn trees."

Lonely is the quirt-quirt of the whippoorwill, the song of the grasshopper and the katydid. And there is somethin lonely about dead fodder blades—the way they rake against the wind at night.

"Does God talk, Brother Littlejohn?"

"W'y yes, God talks. Ain't you got no faith?"

"How do you know?"

"Because it is in the Word."

"Be quiet, please."

"It is the wind in the dead fodder."

"Are you sure that is all?"

"Yes."

"No."

"Why no?"

"It is Brother Groan feelin the sperit."

"How do you know?"

"I saw him jump up and down right out there before me."

"I saw him too jump up and down out there in the path. I saw his sleeve catch on the brush. I saw him in the moonlight."

"He is feelin the sperit then."

The peach orchard is not a new set of teeth. Too many of the teeth are gone if each tree is a tooth. Many of them are snaggled teeth too. Brother Groan walks under the peach trees too, and the good teeth and the bad teeth chew at his robe. Brother Groan gets along. The dead leaves hangin to the peach trees are purple. One cannot tell tonight. But come look tomorrow afternoon when the sun is shinin. There are half-dead leaves on the trees and whole-dead leaves on the trees. The wind fingers with the leaves. Brother Groan's sleeve has caught on the tooth of a peach tree. Brother Sluss hurries to free him. The sleeve is free now. The disciples move on. Brother Groan is silent.

"Where are we goin, Brother Shinliver?"

"To the Kale Nelson Graveyard."

"What for?"

"Brother Groan is goin to show us the Faith in the Word."

"How?"

"I don't know."
"By the Word?"
"No!"
"How?"
"I told you once I didn't know."
"Is that you talkin, Brother Redfern?"
"No."
"I thought I heard somebody."
"That was the wind you heard."
"Yes, that was the wind."
"Yes, that was the wind in the peach-tree leaves."
"Ain't we about there?"
"About where?"
"Kale Nelson Graveyard?"
"Right up there!"
"Right up where?"
"Right up there—see them white tombstones! That is the Kale Nelson Graveyard."

The moon is high above the Kale Nelson Graveyard and the wind is down close to the earth on this high flat. The dead weeds rattle. The dead grass is whisperin somethin. Maybe it is: "The dead lie buried here. The dead of ever-so-long-ago. They lie buried here under our roots. We know the dead lie buried here." The loose leaves rustle in the wind. The moon is still big as a pumpkin floatin in the pretty night sky. The moon is still the color of the insides of a pumpkin.

Across the bones of the old house, Groan and his disciples go. The myrtle is vined around the old logs. There is a pile of stones here, a pile of stones over there. Here is the butt of an old field-stone chimney. There is a gatepost half-rotted. Ramble rose vines climb halfway up the rotted post. Here is a bushy-top yard tree with hitchin rings stapled in the sides. Here is a patch of blackberry briars. The wind blows through the blackberry briars and the blackberry briars scratch the wind. You ought to hear this wind whistle when it is scratched by the briars. If the wind dies, it cannot be buried here where the dead weeds whisper: " The dead lie under our roots, here in the Kale Nelson Graveyard." If Brother Groan dies, he can be buried here. Brother Groan is the kind of dead, when he does die, a grave can hold. Listen: Brother Groan is goin to speak now: "Gather around me, ye men of the Faith. Gather around me, ye men of God. Gather around me here. I want to show you there is power in the Word. Gather around me and let your voices speak in the Unknown Tongue to God."

Here on the myrtle-mantled logs of the old Abraham's house, men are groanin—men are cryin to God. They are pleadin to God. They are mutterin quarter words, half words and whole words to God. It is in the Unknown Tongue. Brother Sluss is on the ground now. He rolls out into the graveyard. He breaks down the dead weeds that just awhile ago whispered to the wind that the dead lay under their roots. Brother Sluss smashes weeds half-dead like a barrel of salt rollin over them. Brother Sluss is a barrel-bellied man. He rolls like a barrel. Brother Littlejohn's pants have slipped below his buttocks. Brother Shinliver is holdin to a tombstone and jerkin. Brother Frazier is pattin the ground with his shovel hands and cryin to God. Brother Groan is cryin to God. He faces the yellow moon and cries to God. "Come around me, men, come around me, you men of Faith, and listen to the Word. I aim to show you what the Faith in the Word will do. It will lift mountains. It will put life back into the dead bodies on this hill here tonight. Here are the dead beneath these weeds and the dead leaves. And one of these dead shall breathe the breath of life before mornin. Brother Sluss, get up off the ground and go right out there to that chimney butt, look under the jam rock where the pothooks used to swing and bring me that coal pick, that corn scoop and that long-handled shovel."

"Where did you say to go, Brother Groan?"

"Out there and look in the butt of that chimney."

"Out there by the blackberry briars, Brother Groan? I'm worked up with the sperit."

"What are you goin to do, Brother Groan?"

"Through me, Brother Redfern, God is goin to give new life to a dead woman this very night."

"Who, Brother Groan?"

"My dead wife."

"Your wife!"

"Yes, my dead wife. What do you think I brought this bundle of clothes along for? They are the old clothes she left in the shack when she died. She is goin to walk off this hill tonight with me. She is goin to live again through the Faith in the Word. It will put new life into the dead. It will lift mountains. You see, Brother Sluss come here with me a year ago today when my wife was buried here on this hill. You remember my wife, don't you, Brother Sluss?"

"Yes, I remember your wife. I was by her bedside prayin when she died. I heard her last breath sizzle. I heard her say, 'I see the blessed Saviour.' Then she was gone. I followed Joe Mangle's mules that pulled her here that muddy September day last year. When your wife died, I thought I'd have to die too. I just couldn't hardly stand it. You had a good woman."

"That cold rainy day was the day I waited till they had all gone off'n the hill but the gravediggers. And when they was throwin over her some of the last dirt, I watched them from behind the butt of that old chimney there in the blackberry vines—I was scrounched down there in that hole where the pot-hooks used to swing. And when one of the gravediggers said: 'Boys, since we're so nearly done and the weather's so rainy and cold, what's you fellars say let's slip down yander behind the bank and take a drink of licker? Looks purty bad to drink here over this woman's dead body and her a woman of God's, but a little licker won't go a bit bad now.' And they all throwed their shovels and picks down and took off over the bank. While they was down over the bank, I slipped out beside the grave and took a long-handled shovel, a corn scoop and a coal pick—I had this in mind when I hid, if they ever left their tools. I wanted to see them throw the dirt in and I didn't want them to see me. I hid the tools in the butt of the chimney where I was hidin. And I said to myself, 'I'll come back here a year from today and I'll put new breath in her through the Faith in the Word.' So, I got the tools. I hid them right here. I stayed with them. The boys couldn't find their tools and they argued how funny it was their tools disappeared so suddenly, said it was such a strange thing. Some men accused the other men of not bringin their tools. They throwed in the rest of the dirt on my dead wife, then they swaggered full of licker off'n the hill. A red leaf stuck to the long-handle shovel handle. I think it was a leaf blowed off'n that sweet-gum tree right over there. There was death in that leaf, same as there was death in my wife. Dead leaves are on the ground tonight, not red with death so much as they was red with death last September in the rain when my wife was buried here."

"Brother Groan, I knowed your wife. She was a fine woman, wasn't she."

"Yes. My wife was a very fine woman."

"Brother Groan, I knowed your wife since you spoke about her. Your wife had a harelip, didn't she? She was marked with a rabbit, wasn't she?"

"Yes, Brother Redfern, my wife had a harelip. But she wasn't marked with no rabbit. God put it there for the sins of her people. And my wife wouldn't let no doctor sew it up. My wife would say in church, 'God put this harelip on me for the sins of my people and I shall wear it for God.' My wife was a good woman."

"Brother Groan, I remember the woman with the harelip. And she was your wife! Well, I saw her five summers ago, a tall woman, slim as a bean pole, with a harelip. I saw her in Puddle, West Virginia. She was in God's house and she said the words you said that she always said about her lip. And one thing she said has always stuck with me. It was somethin like this: 'A man swimmed out in the river with his two sons. He was a good swimmer and they tried to follow him. He led the way for them. One went under the water and never come up again. The father started back with his other son toward the river bank and under he went too, never to come up again. 'My God Almighty,' the father cried out, 'my sons are lost. They went the wrong way too far and I led them. I led them into this danger.' And your wife fairly preached there that night. And the sperit of God was there in that house."

"Brother Groan, I was in Venom, Kentucky, two summers ago and I saw your wife. She was in God's house there. She had a harelip, I remember, and all her teeth nearly showed in front. They looked like awful long teeth. I remember when she was talkin to God she had a awful hard time sayin her words to God. She got up and said the words you said she said about her lip to the people, then she pulled her sleeve up and showed where she was marked on the arm by the belly of a sow. There was a patch of black sow-belly skin on her arm and thin sow-belly hairs scattered all over it. And there was three small sow's teats about the size of a gilt sow's teats. And your wife said: 'People, God has marked me because my people have sinned against God and I am to carry the marks of my sinnin people. I aim to carry the marks too. No doctor can cut the one off'n my arm or sew the one up on my lip.' Brother Groan, your wife was a good woman."

"Yes, Brother Littlejohn, my wife was a good woman."

"Brother Groan, I remember your wife. I saw her in God's house. It has been three years ago this September. I saw her at a tent meetin at Beaverleg, Ohio. And I'll die rememberin one good thing I heard your wife get up and say. She said: 'Women, if I had a man mean as the very Devil, which I ain't got, I would get up and cook for him at the blackest midnight. I would get a good warm meal for him if I had the grub to cook for him. Why? Because where he is goin after he leaves this world—there he won't have no sweet wife to cook for him.' Yes, I remember your wife sayin these words. She had a hard time speakin her testimony to God, for her words was not plain. I remember your wife and the half words she said. It was September in a hayfield near Beaverleg, Ohio, where the tent of God was. Your wife was a good woman, wasn't she?"

"Yes, my wife was a good woman, Brother Pigg. She was a good woman. You are goin to see my wife again. She is goin to walk off this hill with me. You bring the corn scoop here and shovel down through the loose dirt on top of the grave far down as you can shovel and lift out with the short-handle corn scoop. Here is the place. Start right here. Here is the place my wife was buried a year ago today. Yes, my wife was a good woman."

"Did you say to begin here, Brother Groan?"

"Yes, begin right there."

"Right at her feet?"

"I don't like to do this—mess with the dead."

"Ain't you got no Faith?"

"Faith in what?"

"Faith in the Word?"

"Yes, I got Faith in the Word."

"Dig then!"

"Well."

The moist September grave dirt is scooped out like loose corn out of a wagon bed. When the scoops of dirt hit the dirt pile, they are like so many dish rags hittin the kitchen floor. Dirt hits the dead weeds and the dead leaves on the ground in little thuds. The big moon is yellow above the dead dirty grass and the white tombstones and the rain-cloud gray tombstones. The disciples are silent now except for the wet dirt piece-meal hitting the ground. Brother Fain Groan is whisperin to God.

"I need the long-handle shovel!"

"Here is the shovel, Brother Pigg. Leave me dig a little while, Brother Pigg. Ain't you about fagged out?"

"Brother Littlejohn, I believe I will let you spell me a little."

"You have sure scooped this down some, Brother Pigg."

"I raised enough sweat. Closed in down here and the wind don't hit you right."

"Wind can't hit a body down in this hole, can it?"

"No."

"Boys, I'll know my wife by her lip. Thank God, I ain't ashamed of it neither. She told the people she wasn't ashamed of it. And I ain't ashamed of it neither, thank God. God don't heal this old clay temple of ours only through the Faith in the Word. I'll put breath back in my dead wife's body and she'll become my livin wife again. My wife—you have seen my wife and you'll know my wife when she is risen from the grave, Brother Sluss, and breathes the breath of life again."

Brother Groan walks out among the graves. His face is turned toward the stars. He whispers unknown syllables to the wind. The wind whispers unknown syllables to the weeds and to the dead leaves.

"I thought I heard a voice."

"A voice!"

"Yes."

"Ah!"

"The voice of God."

"No."

"It was the voice of the wind."

"Yes."

"The wind."

"The wind in the dead grass."

"Well then, did you hear the voice?"

"No."

"What did you hear?"

"I heard the wind in the grass."

"The wind!"

"Yes. The wind. The wind."

"You are gettin way down there, Brother Littlejohn. Let me spell you a little while with that shovel."

"All right, Brother Redfern. The ground is gettin hard here. Bring the coal pick down with you."

"Did you know there is a slip on one side of this grave? There is a hole down in this grave like a water seep. That is what made the shovelin easy. That is why we are gettin along fast."

"Is it?"

"Yes."

"Throw me down the pick, Brother Pigg. I have found some white tangled roots down here. Wait! I may be able to pull them out with my hand. A root this big, down this far in the ground—I don't see any close trees—it must have come from that wild-cherry standin over there on this side of the blackberry patch."

"Can you yank them roots out with your hands or do you want the coal pick? The ax end of the coal pick will cut them."

"Wait! I'm stung. The root flew up and hit my arm. Wait! Stung again. Wait! Here it comes. May be a snake! My God Almighty, but I'm stung. It can't be a snake though—a snake this deep down!"

"I'll see if it is a root. If it is a wild-cherry root it is a chubby wild-cherry root nearly as big as a two-year old baby's thigh. My God, but it has stung me. It jumped and stung me. I am bit by a snake and you are bit by a snake. Yes. It is a snake. Strike a match! Watch—it is goin to strike again. Watch out. There! See it strike. It is a rusty-mouth grave copperhead. My God!"

"Come out of the grave, Brother Redfern. You have been bit by a rusty-mouth grave copperhead."

"Let us have Faith in the Word."

"Give me your pocketknife, Brother Littlejohn."

"What for?"

"To cut out the bite and suck the blood."

"Ain't you got no Faith in the Word?"

"Yes, but I know what to do for a copperhead bite. We ain't no business here messin with the dead nohow. It is against the Word to prank with the dead. Don't the Word say, 'Let the dead rest. Bury the dead and let them rest'? Give me that knife."

"Brother Redfern, I'll cut your arm on the copperhead bite and suck your blood and you cut my arm on the copperhead bites and suck my blood."

"All right."

"God, ain't this awful out here this night."

"Brother Pigg is bit. Brother Redfern is bit."

"Go down in the grave, Brother Shinliver."

"Are you afraid to go? We're bit and we can't go back. We're goin to get sick in a few minutes."

"I thought I heard a voice."

"You did."

"Yes. Is it God's voice?"

"No. It is the voice of Brother Groan."

"See him! He has opened the bundle of clothes he brought. He is holdin up a woman's dress he brought in the bundle of clothes he carried up here on the hill tonight. He brought them clothes to dress his wife in when we get her dug out'n the grave."

"New clothes?"

"I'll ask and see."

"No—the clothes she used to wear. The dress Brother Groan liked to see her wear. The dress she looked so pretty in. Here is the hat she wore. It is a high-crowned black hat with a goose plume on the side. And here are the shoes she wore last. They are peaked-toe, patent-leather, low-heeled, button shoes. The clothes are right here for the woman soon as she comes out of the grave and the breath of life goes into her lungs."

"I have hit the wood, men. It is the box. I'll have to shovel the dirt from around the box so we can lift it out. I need hand holts. Wait till I clear some of the dirt away with my hands. I'm stung—stung like a red wasper stings right in the calf of the leg. Its teeth are hung in my pants leg. Get me out, men—get me out quick—it is another copperhead."

"Leave him out of the grave, men. See it. It is a copperhead. Its fangs are hung in his pants leg. Hit it with the shovel handle. Cut it with a knife. Kill it!"

"Cut the calf of my leg, Brother Littlejohn, with your pocketknife and suck blood, for I can't get to my leg to suck the blood out and the blood won't come out fast enough unless it is sucked out."

"All right."

"Strike a match. It is a she-copperhead. Its head ain't as copper as the he-copperhead's. I thought it must be a she, for the old rusty-mouthed one was the he-copperhead."

"Ain't you got no Faith in the Word, Brother Shinliver?"

"Yes, but Brother Littlejohn, we ain't got no business messin with the dead. The Word says, 'We must bury the dead and bury them so deep and leave them alone.' Don't the Word say that? I don't want my leg rottin off. Cut my leg and suck the blood."

"All right."

"I got that copperhead."

"Strike a match."

"See how gray the belly is turned up. It looks like a poplar root."

"Are you afraid of that grave, Brother Littlejohn?"

"No, I ain't afraid of that grave."

"Get down and shovel awhile then."

"You want the coal pick?"

"Yes, the coal pick."

"God—God, I'm stung. The first pop out'n the box and I'm

stung right on the soft part of the jaw. The sting was like the sting of a red wasper."

"You stung, Brother Littlejohn?"

"Stung! Yes! My God! Take it off! Take it off! Its fangs are fastened in my flesh. Take it off, men. Take it off!"

"Yank him out'n the hole, men. All right. Come, Brother Frazier."

"Cut that snake off with your pocketknife. Cut it through the middle and it'll let loose. I've heard they wouldn't let loose till it thundered, but cut its guts out with a knife and it'll let loose, I'll bet you a dollar."

"Wait, I'll get it. Got it. Feel its fangs leaving your jaw?"

"No. My jaw is numb."

"Cut his jaw, Brother Frazier, and suck the blood."

"All right."

"You're hit awful close the eye."

"Makes no difference. Cut the bite and suck out the blood."

"Let me down in that grave, I'll take that coffin out by myself. I ain't afraid of no copperhead. No grave copperhead can faze me."

And Brother Frazier, short and stocky two-hundred-and-fifty-pounder, goes down into the grave. He is a mountain of a man. He lifts one end of the box, coffin and dead woman; he lifts it from the gluey earth. He lifts one end out and puts it upon the grave. The other end of the box rests down in the hole.

Brother Pigg and Brother Redfern are gettin mighty sick. They were bitten by the first copperhead, the rusty-mouthed grave he-copperhead. Brother Redfern and Brother Pigg are down under the hill by the wire fence. They are wallowin on the weeds. They are sick enough to die. They have a very high fever, the arm of each man is swollen and numb. They do not know they are wallowing on the weeds in the graveyard. They know no more than the dead beneath them.

Brother Groan comes up with the button shoes, the dress with the white dots, the black high-crowned hat with the white goose plume. Brother Fain Groan does not have a screw driver to take the coffin out of the box and the woman out of the coffin that the mountain of a man Brother Frazier lifted out of the grave hole alone. Brother Fain Groan grabs the coal pick. The box boards fly off one by one—these water-soaked coffin box boards. They are all off. Here is the color of an autumn-seasoned beechstump coffin, rather slim and long the coffin is—but Sister Groan was tall and slender as a bean pole, remember. Brother

Groan doesn't have a screw driver and he puts the sharp end of the coal pick under the coffin lid and he heaves once—only a screak like the tearin off of old clapboards pinned down with rusty square-wire nails. Another heave and another heave, still another and another—off comes the lid.

"My God Almighty. My wife. My God! My wife! Oh my God, but it is my wife. Perfectly natural too! My God! Oh my God Almighty! My wife!" Brother Groan just wilts over like a tobacco leaf in the sun. He wilts beside his dead wife. She wilted one year ago. The whole night and the copperheads is nothin to him now. The night is neither dark nor light to him. He knows no more than the dead woman beside him.

"That's Groan's wife all right. See that lip, Brother Sluss."

"Yes, that is Brother Groan's wife all right. Strike a match. See that arm where it is crossed on her breast. That is Brother Groan's wife all right, Brother Frazier."

"She looks like a rotten black-oak stump since the wind hit her on the face, don't she?"

"She looked like a seasoned autumn-beech stump before the wind hit her face, didn't she?"

"Yes, she did."

"But she looks like a black-oak stump now."

"No. She looks like a wet piece of chestnut bark."

"Ain't it funny the things the wind can do. Change the looks of a person. Talk with God. Whisper around in the corn like Brother Groan whispers to God."

"What is that smells like wild onions in a cow pasture?"

"No, that smell to me is like the sour insides of a dead persimmon tree."

"Let's get away from here. Shake Brother Groan. Get him up and let's go."

"Brother Groan won't wake. See how hard I pull his coat collar. He don't breathe. His heart has quit beatin. Feel! Brother Groan, get up and let's leave here! He's dead, sure as the world. Brother Groan is dead! His breath is gone! Let's get out of here!"

"I tell you, it don't pay to tamper with the dead."

"The Word says the dead shall be at rest. They shall be buried deep enough not to be bothered by men plowin and jolt wagons goin over the tops of them and the cows pickin the grass from over them. The Word says the dead shall rest."

"I think I ruptured a kidney liftin that box out awhile ago by myself. No, it don't pay to tamper with the dead."

Brother Frazier and Brother Sluss walk away from the grave. Brother Frazier walks like a bear. He is a short, broad man. He has to squeeze between some of the tall tombstones. Brother Sluss does not have any trouble. Here is Brother Littlejohn wallowin in the graveyard. He tries to get up and he falls back. He acts like a chicken that has lost its head, but Brother Littlejohn has not lost his head; his head is big and swollen. He does not know any more than the dead beneath him. Here is Brother Shinliver. He lies with his swollen leg propped upon the grave. He, too, is dead, dead as the dead under the ground—dead as Brother Groan, dead as Brother Groan's wife. Brother Pigg and Brother Redfern are lyin lifeless now, lyin down beside the wire fence where one first comes into the graveyard. They were tryin to get home. They couldn't get through four strands of barb wire stretched across the wind. They know no more than the grass beneath them or the dead beneath them. There is vomit all around them on the grass and the dead and the half-dead weeds and the dead leaves. Brother Sluss and Brother Frazier leave the graveyard. They are afraid. They leave the dead there and the sick there with the dead. They go down through the peach orchard, the corn patch, the pig lot and the cow pasture. They are crossin the cow pasture now—down the path where the pawpaw bushes trim each side of the path. Brother Frazier says: "Brother Groan died beside of his dead wife. Or was that put-on, do you suppose? Was he in a trance or was he dead?"

"No, Brother Groan is dead. His heart stopped beatin and I suppose he is dead. I guess that kills the old clay temple when the heart stops beatin."

"I don't believe Brother Groan had the right kind of Faith in the Word."

"Let your wife die and be dead a year. Go at midnight and dig her up and look at her and let the moon shine down on them lip-uncovered front teeth of hers and see what it does to you. See if your heart beats. See the pure natural bloom on her face at first. Strike a match and see the wind turn it black right before your eyes while the match is still burnin and you'd forget all about the Faith in the Word."

"Yes, I saw that. I got sick too. I tell you it don't pay to dig up the dead. The Word says the dead shall have their rest. The Word says the dead die to rest, that they shall be buried deep enough to get their rest without bein bothered by cattle pickin grass from over them, wagons makin tracks over them, men walkin over them. Then we go out and dig up Brother Groan's wife. It is the Word that filled that grave with copperheads. The copperheads was put in there for a purpose when Brother Groan hid in that chimney butt and hid them tools in there that he stole from the grave diggers. We have worked against the Word."

"I got awful sick there at the grave when the coffin was opened and I saw Groan's wife. Lord, I got sick when I saw that mark on her arm—looked plain-blank like the belly of a young sow. I saw the lip too—a three-cornered lip and it black as a last year's corn shuck. It had long white teeth beneath it and one could see the roots of her front teeth. And then her face was the color of a rotten stump. I saw the face turn black as the match stem burned up in the wind. Lord, I had to leave."

"It wasn't the looks that made me sick. It was that awful scent when the coffin was opened. I smelled somethin like mushrooms growin on an old log—a old sour log where the white-bellied water dogs sleep beneath the bark."

"Smelled like wild onions to me."

"I don't believe that Brother Groan had the right kind of Faith. I have never thought it since we was all supposed to meet down there at the Manse Wiffard Gap at that sycamore tree. We was to crucify Brother Groan that night. We was to tie him with a rope to a sycamore limb. And he said his sperit would ride to Heaven right before us on a big white cloud. We went down there and waited around nearly all the night and he never did come. I don't believe he had the right kind of Faith in the Word."

The sun is up. The bright rays of sun, semi-golden, fall on the peach-tree leaves. The oak leaves swirl like clusters of blackbirds in the wind—red, golden, scarlet—semi-golden oak leaves the color of the one that stuck to the shovel handle last September. There is fire in the new September day. The wind is crisp to breathe. The tombstones gleam in the sun; the wind has dried the dew off the weeds, the wind has dried and half-dried the vomit on the leaves and on the grass and the vomit that still sticks to the lips of the four senseless yet livin men that lie in the graveyard with the dead.

The neighborhood is astir. They hunt for Fain Groan, Wilkes Redfern, Roch Shinliver, Cy Pigg, Lucas Littlejohn; David Sluss and Elijah Frazier could tell where they are, but they are ashamed. They slipped in at their back doors. They are in bed now sleepin soundly as the dead.

People know here in the neighborhood that Fain Groan has a band of disciples, that they meet two and three times each week in the woods and in old houses; but they have always come in before daylight. The neighborhood is astir.

But Constable Ricks sees somethin from his house. He sees something goin on up at the graveyard. He has seen plenty of buzzards and crows workin on the carcasses of dead horses, but he has never seen such a swarm in all his life as he now sees upon the hill at the graveyard. He sees crows sittin up in the wild-cherry tree—enough of them sittin upon the limbs to break them off. There are the guard crows even. The ground is black with crows. He hears the crows caw-cawin to each other and to the buzzards tryin to fight them back. But they are turkey buzzards and they won't be whipped by cornfield crows. They fluff their wing feathers and their neck feathers right out and, like fightin game roosters, take right after the crows. The crows give back when they see the turkey buzzards comin. They don't give back until then. Crows fly from the ground up into the wild-cherry tree and then back to the ground. They change about, crow-habit; some guard while others eat.

Constable Ricks starts for the Kale Nelson Graveyard. He is ridin a mule. He lopes the mule up the hill. He sees a pile of fresh dirt before he gets there, he sees somethin like a box on top of the ground, somethin like a man, somethin like a pile of clothes. Up to the graveyard and he sees. The crows fly up in a black cloud. The buzzards are very slow about it, but they fly up too. He ties the mule to a fence post. One buzzard alights on the back of the mule and scares him. Constable Ricks rides the mule back fast as the mule can gallop to Coroner Stone's house and calls him from the corn patch. Coroner Stone jumps on the mule behind Constable Ricks. They gallop the mule back to the graveyard. Here are all the crows and buzzards back and more are comin.

When they scare the crows and the buzzards off Brother Groan and Brother Groan's wife, they fly down at the lower end of the graveyard, they fly down to somethin on the ground. Many as can find a place to light on the fence posts. Constable Ricks runs down there and shoos them away and strikes the air at them as they fly with the long-handle shovel he picks up back at the grave. He finds four men on the ground and finds plenty of sun-dried vomit on the leaves and on the dead weeds. Wilkes Redfern, Roch Shinliver, Cy Pigg, Lucas Littlejohn are lyin senseless on the ground. Constable Ricks thinks they are dead the way the crows are tryin to get to them and the way the buzzards are fightin back the crows from them. He goes up and feels over each heart to see if it is beatin. All hearts are beatin. The flesh of each man is cold. The warm September sun has not thoroughly thawed them after the cool night. "Found four men senseless but yet alive, Fred. Come down here. Let's take care of the livin first." Constable Ricks picks up a clod of dirt and he throws it at the crows with intent to kill. The clod goes through the whole flock of crows and does not touch a feather.

Coroner Fred Stone stays with the dead and livin at the graveyard while Constable Ricks jumps on the mule and gallops over the neighborhood to tell that he has found the missin men. Coroner Stone finds the rusty-mouthed copperhead, the she-copperhead and the young copperhead. The snakes are dead, wilted and limber like a dead horseweed in the sun. He knows the four men have been bitten by copperheads down under the hill by the wire fence where one first comes in the graveyard when walkin up the path, and not ridin a mule or bringin a team. He looks at the face of Brother Groan; it is black—black as a wilted pawpaw leaf. It has been picked on by the crows. But picked on is all. His face is old and tough. It is tough as crow meat. Brother Groan's wife's face is the color of a young blackberry sprout hit by a heavy October frost—wilted and soggy black. Her face has been picked on by the crows. Most of it is gone. Coroner Stone looks carefully at the dress with the white dots, the patent-leather low-heeled button shoes, the black high-crowned hat with the white goose plume in the side. They are in Brother Groan's left arm, his arm is wound around them like the short stubby body of a copperhead and his dead fingers clutch them like copperhead's fangs. Before the neighborhood gets back upon the hill and Constable Ricks comes with the spring wagon to haul the four senseless men home, Coroner Stone holds his inquest: "Fain Groan committed suicide when he dug his wife up and looked at her." He said: "I know he planned to dig her up because here are the old clothes I used to see her wear." That was Coroner Stone's duty.

When Constable Ricks comes upon the hill he arrests the dead man. He thinks that is his duty, for he doesn't know much about the Law. He arrests him on the charge of "Public Indecency." Then he says: "My duties have been faithfully performed within the 'sharp eyes' of the Law."

The neighborhood men put Fain Groan's wife back in the coffin and give her a second burial. They hang the copperheads on the fence wires, for they say it is a sign of rain to hang a dead snake on the fence. They throw the four men in the wagon, senseless but livin men—throw them like four barrels of salt, throw in Brother Groan with his loose flowin robe like he was a shock of fodder with loose stalks danglin around the edges, and they hurry them off the hill in the spring wagon.

Quinn Snodgrass claims the body of Fain Groan. Fidas Campbell claims him too. Quinn Snodgrass is the brother of Fain Groan's second wife; Fidas Campbell is the brother of Fain Groan's first wife. His third wife didn't have a brother to claim him as it is the custom to be buried by the first wife and that is in keepin in accordance with the Word. But Quinn Snodgrass got the body of Fain Groan.

It was the first house beside the wagon road and the team pulled up and they carried his body in the house, though his dead body was still under arrest for Public Indecency. That day Quinn shaved the long beard from Fain Groan's face and cut his hair. He pulled the Christlike robe from his body and bathed his body in water heated in the wash kettle, put the moth-eaten minister's suit on him and prepared him for a nice clean burial. Out in the cow shed, hammers and handsaws were kept busy all the time makin his coffin. The next mornin he was hauled in a jolt wagon, with four boys a-sittin on his coffin, to Pine Hill Graveyard and buried beside of his second wife, Symantha Snodgrass. He was still under arrest for Public Indecency for diggin up his wife so the crows and the buzzards could expose her parts.

There was a quarrel between Beadie Redfern and Sibbie Frazier over Fain Groan's wife's clothes that were picked up at the grave upon the hill. Sibbie got the hat and shoes and Beadie got the dress. Men came and claimed the tools and thanked whoever found them. Tim Holmes claimed the long-handle shovel. Carlos Shelton claimed the corn scoop. Bridge Sombers claimed the coal pick. All testified they had been missin since the day they buried Fain Groan's wife the first time, a year ago the day before.

It is tough now to see Cy Pigg and Wilkes Redfern tryin to plow with one arm. Looks like together they would make a good plowin team. Wilkes lost his left arm. Cy lost his right arm. It is horrible to watch Lucas Littlejohn tryin to eat with just one jaw. One can see his teeth grind the food and watch some of it squirm out through the hole in his jaw if one wants to watch it. The doctors couldn't keep the flesh from rottin and fallin out, though pokeberry roots and sweet milk did heal him. And there is Roch Shinliver, fat as mud, hobblin around on a wooden leg. People knows his tracks by a big shoe track and a peg hole in the ground. His leg is all there—the bone is there; it has never been taken off where the flesh rotted from the copperhead bite and the muscles rotted and left the white bone.

Hollis Summers

HOW THEY CHOSE THE DEAD

Margaret stuck one candle in the middle of Chip's birthday cake, and I lit it with my cigarette lighter. "Blow, blow, Chip," Margaret said.

But Chip didn't blow. He just held the new plastic ball with both hands and banged it against the tray of his highchair. The bell inside the ball tinkled and Chip laughed. Margaret and I laughed too.

"It's wonderful, isn't it?" I said.

"It's wonderful," Margaret said. She leaned against the sink and watched Chip bang the ball. "He won't ever die, will he? He's so beautiful."

The ball slipped from Chip's hand and clinked onto the floor. It didn't roll far. It only wobbled and the bell rang inside it.

"Damn," I said, and Chip said something that sounded like damn, and then he said, "Car-car."

He never did get the idea of blowing out the candle. Once during lunch he put his chin in the icing and drew back as if he'd been burned. We laughed at that too. The frosting was like lather on his face; he licked his lips and laughed with us and said, "Car-car."

"Chip wants to take a long, long ride," Margaret said. "That's what you want, isn't it, Chip? For a birthday present."

Chip banged the blue plastic ball and the bell rang and we got ready to take the long, long ride. I put Chip's mattress in the back of our coupé. I covered the mattress with a sheet and tucked in the corners as if it were a hospital bed. Margaret fixed part of the birthday dinner for a picnic. She had fried chicken and the first tomatoes from our garden and cans of liver and spinach and custard. "And he'll have cake for dessert," Margaret said. "Cake, Chip, you hear that?"

She forgot the diapers and we had to turn around at the edge of town and come back. I wasn't even annoyed with her for forgetting, and she said that I drove better than she did.

"I'm glad we got to see our house again anyhow," Margaret said. "I'm not sorry about leaving the diapers."

"It's a beautiful house," I said.

Chip stood up on his mattress and pressed his face against the back window. He beat the blue ball against the glass.

"Chip's glad we came back. He never heard of its being bad luck."

The motor of the car sounded good. I was listening to the motor. "It's never been bad luck," I said after a minute. "And we're always forgetting things."

"I love you," Margaret said. "I love you and Chip."

"I love you and Chip." I rolled the window up so that there wouldn't be too much air in the back.

Neither of us has any idea how far we drove. I keep trying to visualize the mileage numbers under the speedometer, but nothing comes. We know, of course, that we passed through Carrollton, and that's twenty-three miles from home. It was just two o'clock in Carrollton. The clock over the courthouse said so.

I said, "It's time for his nap, isn't it?"

And Margaret said, "You don't have naps on your birthday, you ought to know that."

Chip came over in the front seat with us. He sat between us and began a lot of talk without words. He didn't look sleepy.

I drove around the courthouse a couple of times and then turned right and went over a bridge. We're both sure we went over a bridge, even though we didn't think anything about it at the time. In a little while we hit a macadam road that had sugar maples along the sides. The road was a cave. The sun shone through the leaves and ran ahead of us. I don't remember being conscious of any fields beyond the trees.

"Maybe we'll come across some place that's just terrific," Margaret said.

"It's pretty, isn't it?"

"Like a bad painting." Margaret began to hum to herself. Chip leaned against her, but he didn't go to sleep. The trees stopped for a while and then they started again. I remember that I kept wondering what it would be like to hear a love song when you were an old man. I wondered if it would be like anything. I started to ask Margaret about it, and then I didn't.

It was probably about three o'clock when we reached the park. My wristwatch had stopped, and I didn't bother to wind it. The time didn't matter.

Margaret sat up suddenly. "What did I tell you? Something terrific."

"You been asleep?"

"No, of course not."

"Damn," Chip said, or something that sounded like it.

The name of the place was Highland Park. We're sure of that. The letters were written over the entrance in electric bulbs. We noticed when we left that one of the bulbs in the G had burned out. I swung the car under the bulbs that spelled HIGHLAND PARK. A man at the gate came out and smiled at us.

"Thirty cents. A dime for each rider and a dime for the car." The man spoke slowly as if he had all of the time in the world.

"But there are three of us." I nodded at Chip. He sat up and blinked his eyes. The side of his face was red and there was perspiration around the line of his hair.

"You got a fine boy," the man said. "No charge for him."

"But we want to pay for him," Margaret said. "It's his birthday."

"No charge." The man gave me my change, a Franklin half dollar and two dimes. I made the car follow some arrows to the parking place.

"It's funny. I wanted to pay for him too," I said.

"We will." Margaret patted her handkerchief around Chip's forehead and neck. "Chip will be a big boy and someday . . ." She wasn't thinking about what she was saying because she stopped and said, "Look, Chip, a swimming pool. A wonderful big swimming pool."

"What do you think of that, Chip?"

"I wonder why nobody's ever told us about this place." Right away Margaret began taking off Chip's clothes.

There wasn't any charge for Chip again, even though we explained about its being his birthday. I told Margaret I'd take him with me, since I dressed faster than she did. Chip wore a pair of training pants. He looked pretty proud of himself. I put him in the wire basket which the desk man had given me. Chip's eyes were big and he said, "Water." Then he said something that sounded like "Oogle," and I said it back to him. We had quite a conversation while I got into the rented trunks.

"Bye," Chip said, and I said, "Bye."

"You're crazy about that kid, aren't you?" A man spoke behind me. I turned around quickly because I had thought we were the only people in the dressing room. The man wore white swimming trunks and his skin was very brown.

"He's a good guy," I told the man. "This is his birthday."

"You can tell that all right," the man said.

I slipped the elastic identification bracelet around my ankle, and took Chip out of the basket. "Is the water good?"

"The water's fine." The man had disappeared by the time I turned to take my clothes back to the desk. I could hear his feet splash through the antiseptic trough outside the dressing room.

The concrete floor was slick. I slipped once. I held to Chip. He laughed as if we had a joke.

Maragret was waiting for us. "Now who dresses fast?" She stood at the edge of the sand which led to the pool. She pulled at the sides of a white bathing cap, and she ran ahead of us over the sand. I was surprised at how much sand they had around the pool. It was like a regular beach. Margaret looked wonderful in the rented bathing suit. It was the color of the yellow sand.

Chip grunted and held to my neck. My shoulder was sunburned from working in the yard and he hurt like the devil. I told him so.

"You know what the last one in is," Margaret shouted. "Hurry!" She beat the water with her hands.

Chip liked the pool right from the first. We stayed in the shallow end the whole time. I don't remember anybody around us, but Margaret says there were some children and a few parents. The place was big though. I told Margaret I ought to go back to the car and get the new ball, but she said there wasn't any need. We took turns swinging Chip through the water.

After a while a wind came up from somewhere. Chip began to shiver a little and we decided it was time to go in. Chip didn't want to get out of the water. He cried and kicked at me, and Margaret kept saying, "Look here, look here, is that our Chip?"

It was almost cold in the dressing room. There wasn't anybody at the desk so I reached over the counter and got the wire basket. A couple of towels with HIGHLAND PARK written on them lay on top of our clothes. The G was blurred. I dried Chip as well as I could. "Look here, look here," I kept saying. I slapped my foot down against the floor and splashed water. The floor was covered with water now. I wondered at the time if the wind had driven the water out of the pool. Chip sniffed and chewed at his upper lip.

But when we met Margaret we forgot about the wind. We took our picnic basket to a table which was shaded by a red and white umbrella. Chip sat in Margaret's lap. "What shall we have for the birthday boy?" Margaret asked. Chip was frowning and then he began to laugh. He said, "Water," and he patted Margaret's arm with his hand.

I ordered a couple of beers and Margaret asked the waiter if it would be too much trouble to fix the juice of two oranges, no water, and to sterilize the glass. The waiter said it wouldn't be any trouble at all. Generally, when we had Chip out we looked around to see who was watching—that's the way we judged people: if they smiled at Chip they were good characters. But we didn't look at anybody that afternoon in Highland Park. The table was an island. We talked about things which we both knew well. I didn't pay for the orange juice—that came to me only yesterday. I had looked at the bill that afternoon too. I had noticed that it was written in a small backhand, like a woman's writing. I thought at the time that it would be a crazy joke if God turned out to be a woman.

When we finished eating, we walked around a little. Highland Park was big. It seemed to stretch clear to the edge of the land. There was a pavilion for dancing. The orchestra men were already standing at the gate. They wore white suits and dark blue ties. There was even a theater with "Air Cooled" on the marquee in letters that were covered with snow. We couldn't know what time it was, but we knew it was getting late.

"We have time for a ride, though, don't we?" I said.

"Maybe one. Would you like to take a fun ride, Chip?"

Chip rubbed his eyes with the back of his hand. He looked shy. He had just started looking shy that week.

We decided on the ferris wheel. It was big, like everything in Highland Park, but it moved slowly, the way a sleepy mind moves. I didn't even try to pay Chip's fare to the man who stood at the bottom of the wheel. We told Chip to notice the bulbs, no bigger than Christmas tree lights, that outlined the spokes of the wheel. Chip looked at them, but he didn't say anything.

It was a long ride for eleven cents. The man who pressed the stick smiled at us every time we curved down past him. He was a big man, and he reminded me of the fellow in the white trunks at the bathhouse, or the waiter, but I can't remember his face. Margaret thinks that his eyes were dark, but I can't remember his eyes.

Once the wheel stopped when we were at the very top. Chip pushed against the rail which fastened us in. It was light still, but suddenly the bulbs on the wheel blinked on. They were blinding at first. I couldn't see anything but the lights which were threaded through the wheel. After a minute the Park beneath us came back into place. The bulbs were in soft colors and Chip tried to reach for them.

"We have to get home, don't we, I guess?" Margaret said. She spoke loudly, as if she had to shout above the soft light. I nodded to her. "We're going to have to go home," she said to the man as we swung past him.

The man smiled. He took us around another time, and then the wheel stopped and the seat we were in rocked back and forth like a cradle.

"Thank you very much," Margaret said. "Very fine ride."

"Thanks," Chip said, or something that sounded like it.

The man did not speak. We are sure of that.

When we passed the theater two young people were dancing in the foyer to a kind of Negro spiritual with a heavy rhythm background. It seemed strange for them to be dancing to a hymn. Margaret said that it seemed strange to her too.

Chip was sound asleep before we got to the car. I laid him on his mattress. Margaret and I stood and watched him, our arms around each other. He rolled over once and then he settled on his back, gone to the world. His right arm was thrown above his head, and the fingers of his hands were loose.

"Don't you wish you could sleep like that?" I said.

"Don't I?" Margaret said. I didn't know what she meant.

I helped her in the car and closed the door carefully. Then I got in on my side and started the engine and eased out of the parking lot. No one was at the gate. Margaret said that we had forgotten to bring a blanket. "But we didn't forget much, did we?" She was whispering.

"Not much," I said, and we both laughed.

Margaret stood on her knees and covered Chip with one of the diapers from the basket. "Do you mind putting your window up?" she said. "The air's stronger back there."

I put the window up and we started through the cave of trees. I pulled at Margaret's shoulder and she moved over beside me. "Yeah," I said.

"It's not like any day, is it?"

"That's right."

The road curved. Margaret leaned forward. "You'd think we could see the lights from the Park, wouldn't you?"

"Maybe we've come too far."

Once Margaret said, "I hope I remembered to turn off the gas under the water heater," and once I asked her if she wanted a cigarette, and once she read a highway sign aloud, "Slow Cattle Crossing." I don't remember anything else we said until just before the city limit of Carrollton. Margaret spoke so softly that I didn't hear her at first; "I guess nobody could write *Pilgrim's Progress* anymore, could they?"

"Could *he*." Margaret looked up at me. She did not smile.

"Sure, sure," I said.

"No, I mean really." Margaret moved away from me. The courthouse was lit up as if it were a funeral parlor or a part of Highland Park.

"There's no point in trying to scare ourselves."

Margaret did not answer.

Beside us was a White Castle hamburger place. Ahead, a street light changed from green to red. A policeman stood on the corner.

I asked, "You want something else to eat?"

"What about Chip?" Margaret placed her hand on the back of the seat to turn around.

"We'll eat in the car." I put on the brakes. Margaret almost lost her balance. "Sorry," I said.

"Why don't you just back up?"

"Isn't there a fireplug?"

"Not much of a one." Margaret was on her knees.

"But there's much of a cop. We'll go around the block." I hummed a tune under my breath. I switched on the dims. The policeman looked at us.

"Chip!" Margaret called.

"Careful, you'll wake him." The light turned to green.

Margaret sucked in her breath. She put her hand on my shoulder. Her hand hurt my shoulder.

"What's the matter with you?" I turned my head. Margaret's face was green in the light. Her eyes were wide and her mouth was opened.

"He's not back here." Margaret spoke softly. The policeman motioned to me. "Chip's not back there."

I reversed the car to the curb beside the fireplug. A sign said, "No Parking Within Ten Feet."

Margaret clicked the light above her head. I put my elbow on the back of the seat, and I leaned on my elbow, and I looked at the mattress. The sheet was rumpled and I could see the outline where Chip's body had been. The plastic ball with the bell inside of it lay in the corner.

I took my left hand and put it on the door handle and pressed down the door handle and the door opened. I stepped down to the ground. I turned around and I pushed back the seat. Chip was not in the car.

The policeman came up to me.

I looked over at Margaret. She lowered her head.

"You havin' some trouble or something?" the policeman said. He was tall and he wore glasses. The right shaft of his glasses was taped with adhesive.

Margaret raised her head. I could see the pulse beating in her throat. "Could you tell us the way to . . . Highland Park?" she asked.

"Highland Park?" The policeman took off his cap. The cap had left a line on his forehead, and above the line were drops of perspiration. "You sure you got the right name?"

"Highland Park," I said.

"There's Melody Park." The policeman nodded. "You take 32 straight out. You can't miss it."

"No, Highland Park," Margaret said. "It's an amusement park. They have a swimming pool, and a theater, and rides."

"There's Melody Park," the policeman said. "But it's not like that. It's a fine place though. They have bands sometimes."

Tears were in Margaret's eyes, but her voice was even. "It's Highland Park we want. HIGHLAND. A bulb is burned out of the G."

"If there was such a place around here, I'd know it, lady. I been born and raised here."

"Well, thank you, then." Margaret pushed back the seat and motioned to me. "We mustn't stay here at the fireplug."

I looked at the policeman for a long time. I couldn't see him very well. I wondered if it were the chlorine in the water that made me not see him very well.

"Melody's a mighty nice place," the policeman said.

Margaret held her hands in her lap. The light from the dashboard showed her hands. She rubbed the nail of her left thumb with the ball of her right thumb.

"God damn." Her words sounded like praying.

But, of course, we couldn't find the road. It was almost daylight when Margaret said, "I guess it doesn't happen to many people . . . this way."

"Margaret?"

"We'd better go home."

She was on her knees. I knew what she was going to reach for. "Please don't. For God's sake, please don't." I didn't mean to shout at her.

She turned around. She hadn't even touched the ball, but the movement of the car made the bell ring.

Robert Penn Warren

THE PATENTED GATE AND THE MEAN HAMBURGER

You have seen him a thousand times. You have seeen him standing on the street corner on Saturday afternoon, in the little county-seat towns. He wears blue jean pants, or overalls washed to a pale pastel blue like the color of sky after a shower in spring, but because it is Saturday he has on a wool coat, an old one, perhaps the coat left from the suit he got married in a long time back. His long wrist bones hang out from the sleeves of the coat, the tendons showing along the bone like the dry twist of grapevine still corded on the stove-length of a hickory sapling you would find in his wood box beside his cookstove among the split chunks of gum and red oak. The big hands, with the knotted, cracked joints and the square, horn-thick nails, hang loose off the wrist bone like clumsy, home-made tools hung on the wall of a shed after work. If it is summer, he wears a straw hat with a wide brim, the straw fraying loose around the edge. If it is winter, he wears a felt hat, black once, but now weathered with streaks of dark gray and dull purple in the sunlight. His face is long and bony, the jawbone long under the drawn-in cheeks. The flesh along the jawbone is nicked in a couple of places where the unaccustomed razor has been drawn over the leather-coarse skin. A tiny bit of blood crusts brown where the nick is. The color of the face is red, a dull red like the red clay mud or clay dust which clings to the bottom of his pants and to the cast-iron-looking brogans on his feet, or a red like the color of a piece of hewed cedar which has been left in the weather. The face does not look alive. It seems to be molded from the clay or hewed from the cedar. When the jaw moves, once, with its deliberate, massive motion on the quid of tobacco, you are still not convinced. That motion is but the cunning triumph of a mechanism concealed within.

But you see the eyes. You see that the eyes are alive. They

are pale blue or gray, set back under the deep brows and thorny eyebrows. They are not wide, but are squinched up like eyes accustomed to wind or sun or to measuring the stroke of the ax or to fixing the object over the rifle sights. When you pass, you see that the eyes are alive and are warily and dispassionately estimating you from the ambush of the thorny brows. Then you pass on, and he stands there in that stillness which is his gift.

With him may be standing two or three others like himself, but they are still, too. They do not talk. The young men, who will be like these men when they get to be fifty or sixty, are down at the beer parlor, carousing and laughing with a high, whickering laugh. But the men on the corner are long past all that. They are past many things. They have endured and will endure in their silence and wisdom. They will stand on the street corner and reject the world which passes under their level gaze as a rabble passes under the guns of a rocky citadel around whose base a slatternly town has assembled.

I had seen Jeff York a thousand times, or near, standing like that on the street corner in town, while the people flowed past him, under the distant and wary and dispassionate eyes in ambush. He would be waiting for his wife and the three tow-headed children who were walking around the town looking into store windows and at the people. After a while they would come back to him, and then, wordlessly, he would lead them to the store where they always did their trading. He would go first, marching with a steady bent-kneed stride, setting the cast-iron brogans down deliberately on the cement; then his wife, a small woman with covert, sidewise, curious glances for the world, would follow, and behind her the towheads bunched together in a dazed, glory-struck way. In the store, when their turn came, Jeff York would move to the counter, accept the clerk's greeting, and then bend down from his height to catch the whispered directions of his wife. He would straighten up and say, "Gimme a sack of flahr, if'n you please." Then when the sack of flour had been brought, he would lean again to his wife for the next item. When the stuff had all been bought and paid for with the grease-thick, wadded dollar bills which he took from an old leather coin purse with a metal catch to it, he would heave it all together into his arms and march out, his wife and towheads behind him and his eyes fixed level over the heads of the crowd. He would march down the street and around to the hitching lot where the wagons were, and put his stuff into his wagon and cover it with an old quilt to wait till he got ready to drive out to his place.

For Jeff York had a place. That was what made him different from the other men who looked like him and with whom he stood on the street corner on Saturday afternoon. They were croppers, but he, Jeff York, had a place. But he stood with them because his father had stood with their fathers and his grandfathers with their grandfathers, or with men like their fathers and grandfathers, in other towns, in settlements in the mountains, in towns beyond the mountains. They were the great-great-great-grandsons of men who, half woodsmen and half farmers, had been shoved into the sand hills, into the limestone hills, into the barrens, two hundred, two hundred and fifty years before and had learned there the way to grabble a life out of the sand and the stone. And when the soil had leached away into the sand or burnt off the stone, they went on west, walking with the bent-kneed stride over the mountains, their eyes squinching warily in the gaunt faces, the rifle over the crooked arm, hunting a new place.

But there was a curse on them. They only knew the life they knew, and that life did not belong to the fat bottom lands, where the cane was head-tall, and to the grassy meadows and the rich swale. So they passed those places by and hunted for the place which was like home and where they could pick up the old life, with the same feel in the bones and the squirrel's bark sounding the same after first light. They had walked a long way, to the sand hills of Alabama, to the red country of North Mississippi and Louisiana, to the Barrens of Tennessee, to the Knobs of Kentucky and the scrub country of West Kentucky, to the Ozarks. Some of them had stopped in Cobb County, Tennessee, in the hilly eastern part of the county, and had built their cabins and dug up the ground for the corn patch. But the land had washed away there, too, and in the end they had come down out of the high land into the bottoms—for half of Cobb County is a rich, swelling country—where the corn was good and the tobacco unfurled a leaf like a yard of green velvet and the white houses stood among the cedars and tulip trees and maples. But they were not to live in the white houses with the limestone chimneys set strong at the end of each gable. No, they were to live in the shacks on the back of the farms, or in cabins not much different from the cabins they had once lived in two hundred years before over the mountains or, later, in the hills of Cobb County. But the shacks and the cabins now stood on somebody else's ground, and the curse which they had brought with them over the mountain trail, more precious than the bullet mold or grandma's quilt, the curse which was the very feeling in the bones and the habit in the hand, had come full circle.

Jeff York was one of those men, but he had broken the curse. It had taken him more than thirty years to do it, from the time when he was nothing but a big boy until he was fifty. It had taken him from sun to sun, year in and year out, and all the sweat in his body, and all the power of rejection he could muster, until the very act of rejection had become a kind of pleasure, a dark, secret, savage dissipation, like an obsessing vice. But those years had given him his place, sixty acres with a house and barn.

When he bought the place, it was not very good. The land was run-down from years of neglect and abuse. But Jeff York put brush in the gullies to stop the wash and planted clover on the run-down fields. He mended the fences, rod by rod. He patched the roof on the little house and propped up the porch, buying the lumber and shingles almost piece by piece and one by one as he could spare the sweat-bright and grease-slick quarters and half-dollars out of his leather purse. Then he painted the house. He painted it white, for he knew that that was the color you painted a house sitting back from the road with its couple of maples, beyond the clover field.

Last, he put up the gate. It was a patented gate, the kind you can ride up to and open by pulling on a pull rope without getting off your horse or out of your buggy or wagon. It had a high pair of posts, well braced and with a high crossbar between, and the bars for the opening mechanism extending on each side. It was painted white, too. Jeff was even prouder of the gate than he was of the place. Lewis Simmons, who lived next to Jeff's place, swore he had seen Jeff come out after dark on a mule and ride in and out of that gate, back and forth, just for the pleasure of pulling on the rope and making the mechanism work. The gate was the seal Jeff York had put on all the years of sweat and rejection. He could sit on the porch on a Sunday afternoon in summer, before milking time, and look down the rise, down the winding dirt track, to the white gate beyond the clover, and know what he needed to know about all the years passed.

Meanwhile Jeff York had married and had had the three towheads. His wife was twenty years or so younger than he, a small, dark woman, who walked with her head bowed a little and from that humble and unprovoking posture stole sidewise, secret glances at the world from eyes which were brown or black—you never could tell which because you never remembered having looked her straight in the eye—and which were surprisingly bright in that sidewise, secret flicker, like the eyes of a small, cunning bird which surprise you from the brush. When they came down to town she moved along the street, with a child in her arms or later with the three trailing behind her, and stole her looks at the world. She wore a calico dress, dun-colored, which hung loose to conceal whatever shape her thin body had, and in winter over the dress a brown wool coat with a scrap of fur at the collar which looked like some tattered growth of fungus feeding on old wood. She wore black high-heeled shoes, slippers of some kind, which she kept polished and which surprised you under that dress and coat. In the slippers she moved with a slightly limping, stealthy gait, almost sliding them along the pavement, as though she had not fully mastered the complicated trick required to use them properly. You knew that she wore them only when she came to town, that she carried them wrapped up in a piece of newspaper until their wagon had reached the first house on the outskirts of town, and that, on the way back, at the same point, she would take them off and wrap them up again and hold the bundle in her lap until she got home. If the weather happened to be bad, or if it was winter, she would have a pair of old brogans under the wagon seat.

It was not that Jeff York was a hard man and kept his wife in clothes that were as bad as those worn by the poorest of the women of the croppers. In fact, some of the cropper women, poor or not, black or white, managed to buy dresses with some color in them and proper hats, and went to the moving picture show on Saturday afternoon. But Jeff still owed a little money on his place, less than two hundred dollars, which he had had to borrow to rebuild his barn after it was struck by lightning. He had, in fact, never been entirely out of debt. He had lost a mule which had got out on the highway and been hit by a truck. That had set him back. One of his towheads had been sickly for a couple of winters. He had not been in deep, but he was not a man, with all those years of rejection behind him, to forget the meaning of those years. He was good enough to his family. Nobody ever said the contrary. But he was good to them in terms of all the years he had lived through. He did what he could afford. He bought the towheads a ten-cent bag of colored candy every Saturday afternoon for them to suck on during the ride home in the wagon, and the last thing before they left town, he always took the lot of them over to the dogwagon to get hamburgers and orange pop.

The towheads were crazy about hamburgers. And so was his wife, for that matter. You could tell it, even if she didn't say anything, for she would lift her bowed-forward head a little, and her face would brighten, and she would run her tongue out to wet her lips just as the plate with the hamburger would be set on the counter before her. But all those folks, like Jeff York and his family, like hamburgers, with pickle and onions and mustard and tomato catsup, the whole works. It is something different. They stay out in the country and eat hog-meat, when they can get it, and greens and corn bread and potatoes, and nothing but a pinch of salt to brighten it on the tongue, and when they get to town and get hold of beef and wheat bread and all the stuff to jack up the flavor, they have to swallow to keep the mouth from flooding before they even take the first bite.

So the last thing every Saturday, Jeff York would take his family over to Slick Hardin's *Dew Drop Inn Diner* and give them the treat. The diner was built like a railway coach, but it was set on a concrete foundation on a lot just off the main street of town. At each end the concrete was painted to show wheels. Slick Hardin kept the grass just in front of the place pretty well mowed and one or two summers he even had a couple of flower beds in the middle of that shirttail-size lawn. Slick had a good business. For a few years he had been a prelim fighter over in Nashville and had got his name in the papers a few times. So he was a kind of hero, with the air of romance about him. He had been born, however, right in town and, as soon as he had found out he wasn't ever going to be good enough to be a real fighter, he had come back home and started the dogwagon, the first one ever in town. He was a slick-skinned fellow, about thirty-five, prematurely bald, with his head slick all over. He had big eyes, pale blue and slick looking like agates. When he said something that he thought smart, he would roll his eyes around, slick in his head like marbles, to see who was laughing. Then he'd wink. He had done very well with his business, for despite the fact that he had picked up city ways and a lot of city talk, he still remembered enough to deal with the country people, and they were the ones who brought the dimes in. People who lived right there in town, except for school kids in the afternoon and the young toughs from the pool room or men on the night shift down at the railroad, didn't often get around to the dogwagon.

Slick Hardin was perhaps trying to be smart when he said what he did to Mrs. York. Perhaps he had forgotten, just for that moment, that people like Jeff York and his wife didn't like to be kidded, at least not in that way. He said what he did, and then grinned and rolled his eyes around to see if some of the other people present were thinking it was funny.

Mrs. York was sitting on a stool in front of the counter, flanked on one side by Jeff York and on the other by the three towheads. She had just sat down to wait for the hamburger—there were several orders in ahead of the York order—and had been watching in her sidewise fashion every move of Slick Hardin's hands as he patted the pink meat onto the hot slab and wiped the split buns over the greasy iron to make them ready to receive it. She always watched him like that, and when the hamburger was set before her she would wet her lips with her tongue.

That day Slick set the hamburger down in front of Mrs. York, and said, "Anybody likes hamburger much as you, Mrs. York, ought to git him a hamburger stand."

Mrs. York flushed up, and didn't say anything, staring at her plate. Slick rolled his eyes to see how it was going over, and somebody down the counter snickered. Slick looked back at the Yorks, and if he had not been so encouraged by the snicker he might, when he saw Jeff York's face, have hesitated before going on with his kidding. People like Jeff York are touchous, and they are especially touchous about the womenfolks, and you do not make jokes with or about their womenfolks unless it is perfectly plain that the joke is a very special kind of friendly joke. The snicker down the counter had defined the joke as not entirely friendly. Jeff was looking at Slick, and something was growing slowly in that hewed-cedar face, and back in the gray eyes in the ambush of thorny brows.

But Slick did not notice. The snicker had encouraged him, and so he said, "Yeah, if I liked them hamburgers much as you, I'd buy me a hamburger stand. Fact, I'm selling this one. You want to buy it?"

There was another snicker, louder, and Jeff York, whose

hamburger had been about half way to his mouth for another bite, laid it down deliberately on his plate. But whatever might have happened at that moment did not happen. It did not happen because Mrs. York lifted her flushed face, looked straight at Slick Hardin, swallowed hard to get down a piece of the hamburger or to master her nerve, and said in a sharp, strained voice, "You sellen this place?"

There was complete silence. Nobody had expected her to say anything. The chances were she had never said a word in that diner in the couple of hundred times she had been in it. She had come in with Jeff York and, when a stool had come vacant, had sat down, and Jeff had said, "Gimme five hamburgers, if'n you please, and make 'em well done, and five bottles of orange pop." Then, after the eating was over, he had always laid down seventy-five cents on the counter—that is, after there were five hamburger-eaters in the family—and walked out, putting his brogans down slow, and his wife and kids following without a word. But now she spoke up and asked the question, in that strained, artificial voice, and everybody, including her husband, looked at her with surprise.

As soon as he could take it in, Slick Hardin replied, "Yeah, I'm selling it."

She swallowed hard again, but this time it could not have been hamburger, and demanded, "What you asken fer hit?"

Slick looked at her in the new silence, half shrugged, a little contemptuously, and said, "Fourteen hundred and fifty dollars."

She looked back at him, while the blood ebbed from her face. "Hit's a lot of money," she said in a flat tone, and returned her gaze to the hamburger on her plate.

"Lady," Slick said defensively, "I got that much money tied up here. Look at that there stove. It is a *Heat Master* and they cost. Them coffee urns, now. Money can't buy no better. And this here lot, lady, the diner sets on. Anybody knows I got that much money tied up here. I got more. This lot cost me more'n . . ." He suddenly realized that she was not listening to him. And he must have realized, too, that she didn't have a dime in the world and couldn't buy his diner, and that he was making a fool of himself, defending his price. He stopped abruptly, shrugged his shoulders, and then swung his wide gaze down the counter to pick out somebody to wink to.

But before he got the wink off, Jeff York had said, "Mr. Hardin."

Slick looked at him and asked, "Yeah?"

"She didn't mean no harm," Jeff York said. "She didn't mean to be messen in yore business."

Slick shrugged. "Ain't no skin off my nose," he said. "Ain't no secret I'm selling out. My price ain't no secret neither."

Mrs. York bowed her head over her plate. She was chewing a mouthful of her hamburger with a slow, abstracted motion of her jaw, and you knew that it was flavorless on her tongue.

That was, of course, on a Saturday. On Thursday afternoon of the next week Slick was in the diner alone. It was the slack time, right in the middle of the afternoon. Slick, as he told it later, was wiping off the stove and wasn't noticing. He was sort of whistling to himself, he said. He had a way of whistling soft through his teeth. But he wasn't whistling loud, he said, not so loud he wouldn't have heard the door open or the steps if she hadn't come gum-shoeing in on him to stand there waiting in the middle of the floor until he turned round and was so surprised he nearly had heart failure. He had thought he was there alone, and there she was, watching every move he was making, like a cat watching a goldfish swim in a bowl.

"Howdy-do," he said, when he got his breath back.

"This place still fer sale?" she asked him.

"Yeah, lady," he said.

"What you asken fer hit?"

"Lady, I done told you," Slick replied, "fourteen hundred and fifty dollars."

"Hit's a heap of money," she said.

Slick started to tell her how much money he had tied up there, but before he had got going, she had turned and slipped out of the door.

"Yeah," Slick said later to the men who came into the diner, "me like a fool starting to tell her how much money I got tied up here when I knowed she didn't have a dime. That woman's crazy. She must walked that five or six miles in here just to ask me something she already knowed the answer to. And then turned right round and walked out. But I am selling me this place. I'm tired of slinging hash to them hicks. I got me some connections over in Nashville and I'm gonna open me a place over there. A cigar stand and about three pool tables and maybe some beer. I'll have me a sort of club in the back. You know, membership cards to git in, where the boys will play a little game. Just sociable. I got good connections over in Nashville.

I'm selling this place. But that woman, she ain't got a dime. She ain't gonna buy it."

But she did.

On Saturday Jeff York led his family over to the diner. They ate hamburgers without a word and marched out. After they had gone, Slick said, "Looks like she ain't going to make the invest-mint. Gonna buy a block of bank stock instead." Then he rolled his eyes, located a brother down the counter, and winked.

It was almost the end of the next week before it happened. What had been going on inside the white house out on Jeff York's place nobody knew or was to know. Perhaps she just starved him out, just not doing the cooking or burning everything. Perhaps she just quit attending to the children properly and he had to come back tired from work and take care of them. Perhaps she just lay in bed at night and talked and talked to him, asking him to buy it, nagging him all night long, while he would fall asleep and then wake up with a start to hear her voice still going on. Or perhaps she just turned her face away from him and wouldn't let him touch her. He was a lot older than she, and she was probably the only woman he had ever had. He had been too ridden by his dream and his passion for rejection during all the years before to lay even a finger on a woman. So she had him there. Because he was a lot older and because he had never had another woman. But perhaps she used none of these methods. She was a small, dark, cunning woman, with a sidewise look from her lowered face, and she could have thought up ways of her own, no doubt.

Whatever she thought up, it worked. On Friday morning Jeff York went to the bank. He wanted to mortgage his place, he told Todd Sullivan, the president. He wanted fourteen hundred and fifty dollars, he said. Todd Sullivan would not let him have it. He already owed the bank one hundred and sixty dollars and the best he could get on a mortgage was eleven hundred dollars. That was in 1935 and then farmland wasn't worth much and half the land in the country was mortgaged anyway. Jeff York sat in the chair by Todd Sullivan's desk and didn't say anything. Eleven hundred dollars would not do him any good. Take off the hundred and sixty he owed and it wouldn't be but a little over nine hundred dollars clear to him. He sat there quietly for a minute, apparently turning that fact over in his head. Then Todd Sullivan asked him, "How much you say you need?"

Jeff York told him.

"What you want it for?" Todd Sullivan asked.

He told him that.

"I tell you," Todd Sullivan said, "I don't want to stand in the way of a man bettering himself. Never did. That diner ought to be a good proposition, all right, and I don't want to stand in your way if you want to come to town and better yourself. It will be a step up from that farm for you, and I like a man has got ambition. The bank can't lend you the money, not on that piece of property. But I tell you what I'll do. I'll buy your place. I got me some walking horses I'm keeping out on my father's place. But I could use me a little place of my own. For my horses. I'll give you seventeen hundred for it. Cash."

Jeff York did not say anything to that. He looked slow at Todd Sullivan as though he did not understand.

"Seventeen hundred," the banker repeated. "That's a good figure. For these times."

Jeff was not looking at him now. He was looking out the window, across the alleyway—Todd Sullivan's office was in the back of the bank. The banker, telling about it later when the doings of Jeff York had become for a moment a matter of interest, said, "I thought he hadn't even heard me. He looked like he was half asleep or something. I coughed to sort of wake him up. You know the way you do. I didn't want to rush him. You can't rush those people, you know. But I couldn't sit there all day. I had offered him a fair price."

It was, as a matter of fact, a fair price for the times, when the bottom was out of everything in the section.

Jeff York took it. He took the seventeen hundred dollars and bought the dogwagon with it, and rented a little house on the edge of town and moved in with his wife and the towheads. The first day after they got settled, Jeff York and his wife went over to the diner to get instructions from Slick about running the place. He showed Mrs. York all about how to work the coffee machine and the stove, and how to make up the sandwiches, and how to clean the place up after herself. She fried up hamburgers for all of them, herself, her husband, and Slick Hardin, for practice, and they ate the hamburgers while a couple of hangers-on watched them. "Lady," Slick said, for he had money in his pocket and was heading out for Nashville on the seven o'clock train that night, and was feeling expansive, "Lady, you sure fling a mean hamburger."

He wiped the last crumbs and mustard off his lips, got his valise from behind the door, and said, "Lady, git in there and pitch. I hope you make a million hamburgers." Then he stepped out into the bright fall sunshine and walked away whistling up the street, whistling through his teeth and rolling his eyes as though there were somebody to wink to. That was the last anybody in town ever saw of Slick Hardin.

The next day, Jeff York worked all day down at the diner. He was scrubbing up the place inside and cleaning up the trash which had accumulated behind it. He burned all the trash. Then he gave the place a good coat of paint outside, white paint. That took him two days. Then he touched up the counter inside with varnish. He straightened up the sign out front, which had begun to sag a little. He had that place looking spic and span.

Then on the fifth day after they got settled—it was Sunday—he took a walk in the country. It was along toward sun when he started out, not late, as a matter of fact, for by October the days are shortening up. He walked out the Curtisville pike and out the cut-off leading to his farm. When he entered the cut-off, about a mile from his own place, it was still light enough for the Bowdoins, who had a filling station at the corner, to see him plain when he passed.

The next time anybody saw him was on Monday morning about six o'clock. A man taking milk into town saw him. He was hanging from the main cross bar of the white patented gate. He had jumped off the gate. But he had propped the thing open so there wouldn't be any chance of clambering back up on it if his neck didn't break when he jumped and he should happen to change his mind.

But that was an unnecessary precaution, as it developed. Dr. Stauffer said that his neck was broken very clean. "A man who can break a neck as clean as that could make a living at it," Dr. Stauffer said. And added, "If he's damned sure it ain't ever his own neck."

Mrs. York was much cut up by her husband's death. People were sympathetic and helpful, and out of a mixture of sympathy and curiosity she got a good starting trade at the diner. And the trade kept right on. She got so she didn't hang her head and look sidewise at you and the world. She would look straight at you. She got so she could walk in high heels without giving the impression that it was a trick she was learning. She wasn't a bad-looking woman, as a matter of fact, once she had caught on how to fix herself up a little. The railroad men and the pool hall gang liked to hang out there and kid with her. Also, they said, she flung a mean hamburger.

POEMS

Harriette Simpson Arnow

ODE TO A PURPLE ALUMINUM CHRISTMAS TREE

Last year when residential streets
with their strings of colored lights
resembled filling stations
and the glitter of shop windows
hurt my eyes,
a woman met in the course of an errand
said:

"Oh, you must go to Mike's
out on Stadium;
you can't imagine the Christmas trees
they have for sale;
all aluminum
but in different colors,
a whole row of big purple ones;
I could stand all day
and just look at them."

I wanted to cry;
instead went home and tried to write
Ode To A Purple Aluminum Christmas Tree.
Trying
was as far as I ever got.

Wendell Berry

THE MAD FARMER REVOLUTION

BEING A FRAGMENT
OF THE NATURAL HISTORY OF NEW EDEN,
IN HOMAGE
TO MR. ED McCLANAHAN, ONE OF THE LOCALS

The mad farmer, the thirsty one,
went dry. When he had time
he threw a visionary high
lonesome on the holy communion wine.
"It is an awesome event
when an earthen man has drunk
his fill of the blood of a god,"
people said, and got out of his way.
He plowed the churchyard, the
minister's wife, three graveyards
and a golf course. In a parking lot
he planted a forest of little pines.
He sanctified the groves,
dancing at night in the oak shades
with goddesses. He led
a field of corn to creep up
and tassel like an Indian tribe
on the courthouse lawn. Pumpkins
ran out to the ends of their vines
to follow him. Ripe plums
and peaches reached into his pockets.
Flowers sprang up in his tracks
everywhere he stepped. And then
his planter's eye fell on
that parson's fair fine lady
again. "O holy plowman," cried she,
"I am all grown up in weeds.
Pray, bring me back into good tilth."

He tilled her carefully
and laid her by, and she
did bring forth others of her kind,
and others, and some more.
They sowed and reaped till all
the countryside was filled
with farmers and their brides sowing
and reaping. When they died
they became two spirits of the woods.

On their graves were written
these words without sound:
"Here lies Saint Plowman.
Here lies Saint Fertile Ground."

Wendell Berry

THE CONTRARINESS OF THE MAD FARMER

I am done with apologies. If contrariness is my
inheritance and destiny, so be it. If it is my mission
to go in at exits and come out at entrances, so be it.
I have planted by the stars in defiance of the experts,
and tilled somewhat by incantation and by singing,
and reaped, as I knew, by luck and Heaven's favor,
in spite of the best advice. If I have been caught
so often laughing at funerals, that was because
I knew the dead were already slipping away,
preparing a comeback, and can I help it?
And if at weddings I have gritted and gnashed
my teeth, it was because I knew where the bridegroom
had sunk his manhood, and knew it would not
be resurrected by a piece of cake. "Dance" they told me,
and I stood still, and while they stood
quiet in line at the gate of the Kingdom, I danced.
"Pray" they said, and I laughed, covering myself
in the earth's brightnesses, and then stole off gray
into the midst of a revel, and prayed like an orphan.
When they said "I know that my Redeemer liveth,"
I told them "He's dead." And when they told me
"God is dead," I answered "He goes fishing every day
in the Kentucky River. I see Him often."
When they asked me would I like to contribute
I said no, and when they had collected
more than they needed, I gave them as much as I had.
When they asked me to join them I wouldn't,
and then went off by myself and did more
than they would have asked. "Well, then" they said
"go and organize the International Brotherhood
of Contraries," and I said "Did you finish killing
everybody who was against peace?" So be it.
Going against men, I have heard at times a deep harmony
thrumming in the mixture, and when they ask me what
I say I don't know. It is not the only or the easiest
way to come to the truth. It is one way.

Wendell Berry

THE BIRTH
(Near Port William)

They were into the lambing, up late.
Talking and smoking around their lantern,
they squatted in the barn door, left open
so the quiet of the winter night
diminished what they said. The chill
had begun to sink into their clothes.
Now and then they raised their hands
to breathe on them. The youngest one
yawned and shivered.

"Damn," he said,
"I'd like to be asleep. I'd like to be
curled up in a warm nest like an old
groundhog, and sleep till spring."

"When I was your age, Billy, it wasn't
sleep I thought about," Uncle Stanley said.
"Last few years here I've took to sleeping."

And Raymond said: "To sleep till spring
you'd have to have a trust in things
the way animals do. Been a long time,
I reckon, since people felt safe enough
to sleep more than a night. You might
wake up someplace you didn't go to sleep at."

They hushed a while, as if to let the dark
brood on what they had said. Behind them
a sheep stirred in the bedding and coughed.
It was getting close to midnight.
Later they would move back along the row

of penned ewes, making sure the newborn
lambs were well dried, and had sucked,
and then they would go home cold to bed.
The barn stood between the ridgetop
and the woods along the bluff. Below
was the valley floor and the river
they could not see. They could hear
the wind dragging its underside
through the bare branches of the woods.
And suddenly the wind began to carry
a low singing. They looked across
the lantern at each other's eyes
and saw they all had heard. They stood,
their huge shadows rising up around them.
The night had changed. They were already
on their way—dry leaves underfoot
and mud under the leaves—to another barn
on down along the woods' edge,
an old stripping room, where by the light
of the open stove door they saw the man,
and then the woman and the child
lying on a bed of straw on the dirt floor.

"Well, look a there," the old man said.
"First time this ever happened here."

And Billy, looking, and looking away,
said: "Howdy. Howdy. Bad night."

And Raymond said: "There's a first
time, they say, for everything."

And that,
he thought, was as reassuring as anything
was likely to be, and as he needed it to be.
They did what they could. Not much.
They brought a piece of rug and some sacks
to ease the hard bed a little, and one
wedged three dollar bills into a crack
in the wall in a noticeable place.
And they stayed on, looking, looking away,

until finally the man said they were well
enough off, and should be left alone.
They went back to their sheep. For a while
longer they squatted by their lantern
and talked, tired, wanting sleep, yet stirred
by wonder—old Stanley too, though he would not
say so.

"Don't make no difference," he said.
"They'll have 'em anywhere. Looks like a man
would have a right to be born in bed, if not
die there, but he don't."

"But you heard
that singing in the wind," Billy said.
"What about that?"

"Ghosts. They do that way."

"Not that way."

"Scared him, it did."
The old man laughed. "We'll have to hold
his damn hand for him, and lead him home."

"It don't even bother you," Billy said.
"You go right on just the same. But you heard."

"Now that I'm old I sleep in the dark.
That ain't what I used to do in it. I heard
something."

"You heard a good deal more
than you'll understand," Raymond said,
"or him or me either."

They looked at him.
He had, they knew, a talent for unreasonable
belief. He could believe in tomorrow
before it became today—a human enough
failing, and they were tolerant.

He said:
"It's the old ground trying it again.
Solstice, seeding and birth—it never
gets enough. It wants the birth of a man
to bring together sky and earth, like a stalk
of corn. It's not death that makes the dead
rise out of the ground, but something alive
straining up, rooted in darkness, like a vine.
That's what you heard. If you're in the right mind
when it happens, it can come on you strong,
and you might hear music passing on the wind,
or see a light where there wasn't one before."

"Well, how do you know if it amounts to anything?"

"You don't. It usually don't. It would take
a long long time to ever know."

But that night
and other nights afterwards, up late,
there was a feeling in them—familiar
to them, but always startling in its strength—
like the thought, on a winter night,
of the lambing ewes dry-bedded and fed,
and the thought of the wild creatures warm
asleep in their nests, deep underground.

Wendell Berry

WATER

I was born in a drouth year. That summer
my mother waited in the house, enclosed
in the sun and the dry ceaseless wind,
for the men to come back in the evenings,
bringing water from a distant spring.
Veins of leaves ran dry, roots shrank.
And all my life I have dreaded the return
of that year, sure that it still is
somewhere, like a dead enemy's soul. Fear
of dust in my mouth is always with me,
and I am the faithful husband of the rain,
I love the water of wells and springs
and the taste of roofs in the water of cisterns.
I am a dry man whose thirst is praise
of clouds, and whose mind is something of a cup.
My sweetness is to wake in the night
after days of dry heat, hearing the rain.

Thomas Merton

THE READER

Lord, when the clock strikes
Telling the time with cold tin
And I sit hooded in this lectern

Waiting for the monks to come,
I see the red cheeses, and bowls
All smile with milk in ranks upon their tables.

Light fills my proper globe
(I have won light to read by
With a little, tinkling chain)

And the monks come down the cloister
With robes as voluble as water.
I do not see them but I hear their waves.

It is winter, and my hands prepare
To turn the pages of the saints:
And to the trees Thy moon has frozen on the windows
My tongue shall sing Thy Scripture.

Then the monks pause upon the step
(With me here in this lectern
And Thee there on Thy crucifix)

And gather little pearls of water on their fingers' ends
Smaller than this my psalm.

Thomas Merton

WISDOM

I studied it and it taught me nothing.
I learned it and soon forgot everything else:
Having forgotten, I was burdened with knowledge—
The insupportable knowledge of nothing.

How sweet my life would be, if I were wise!
Wisdom is well known
When it is no longer seen or thought of.
Only then is understanding bearable.

Thomas Merton

TRAPPISTS, WORKING

Now all our saws sing holy sonnets in this world of
timber
Where oaks go off like guns, and fall like cataracts,
Pouring their roar into the wood's green well.

Walk to us, Jesus, through the wall of trees,
And find us still adorers in these airy churches,
Singing our other Office with our saws and axes.
Still teach Your children in the busy forest,
And let some little sunlight reach us, in our mental
shades, and leafy studies.

When time has turned the country white with grain
And filled our regions with the thrashing sun,
Walk to us, Jesus, through the walls of wheat
When our two tractors come to cut them down:
Sow some light winds upon the acres of our spirit,
And cool the regions where our prayers are reapers,
And slake us, Heaven, with Your living rivers.

Thomas Merton

THE GUNS OF FORT KNOX

Guns at the camp (I hear them suddenly)
Guns make the little houses jump. I feel
Explosions in my feet, through boards.
Wars work under the floor. Wars
Dance in the foundations. Trees
Must also feel the guns they do not want
Even in their core.
As each charge bumps the shocked earth
They shudder from the root.

Shock the hills, you guns! They are
Not too firm even without dynamite.
These Chinese clayfoot hills
Founded in their own shale
Shift their feet in friable stone.

Such ruins cannot
Keep the armies of the dead
From starting up again.
They'll hear these guns tonight
Tomorrow or some other time.
They'll wake. They'll rise
Through the stunned rocks, form
Regiments and do death's work once more.

Guns, I say, this is not
The right resurrection. All day long
You punch the doors of death to wake
A slain generation. Let them lie
Still. Let them sleep on,
O guns. Shake no more
(But leave the locks secure)
Hell's door.

Jim Wayne Miller

THE REVEREND MR. THICK

Commissioned to preach your funeral, the Reverend Mr. Thick,
the one you thought a fool, not looking thinner,
rejoiced in God's great bounty, your daughter's dinner.
He ate, unless I mistake my arithmetic,
four golden drumsticks in quick succession,
three wings, two necks, a gizzard, rolls untold,
then started a story (already we felt consoled),
but had to break it off in a long digression.

Leaning on the lectern, mating trite trope to trope,
backed by the dollars and cents on Sunday's roll,
he plunged us into doubt about your soul;
then when the women wept, he gave us hope.
Just as in life, the calmest man about,
you were the least concerned, the least in doubt.

Jim Wayne Miller

NOVEMBER 1963

Unnatural autumn, strange fall without frost
And cracking cold to fell what creeps and flies,
Freak fall when swollen bullfrogs lust,
Mounting slippery mates with milky eyes,
The dazzled wasp builds low and prophesies
This tilted twisted time of crazed crickets
Pottericking in the mildewed stalls
And sullen desperado yellowjackets
Hovering hungry over cracks in walls.
The hairy-legged hoddlum spider crawls
And hornet-headed death on whining wings
Waits, squinting down in Dallas, holed
In concrete walls, then flying maddened, stings
Now noisy days are by the wasp foretold
And funeral flowers lie black in futile cold.

Jim Wayne Miller

NATURE POEM EMBODYING A TRUTH

Frantic one night for some place to be safe,
a rabbit on his journey through this life
hopped from dusty weeds into the middle
of a highway — just as fourthousandpoundsof metal
came roaring down the lane the rabbit sat in.
The rabbit crouched and felt his long ears flatten.
He looked into the headlights and went blind,
he zig-zagged down the double yellow line,
he stopped, he looked sideways and tried to focus,
hoping to get a bearing on his locus.
Then brilliantly the back part of his brain
called into play all his might and main.
It was as if the tilting strip of asphalt
were the down side of a see-saw used to vault
him vertically into darkness over the glare.
Thus elevated, poised briefly there,
astonished at his own accomplishment,
he found his bearings, made good his descent,
touched the road again and, rubbery, leapt
into the weeds just as the auto swept
past, so close the wake of the rushing air
rippled wave after wave through his fur.
Sitting in the weeds he grew reflective.
"Sometimes darkness puts things in perspective,"
he thought. His heart ticked like a metronome.
He knew he was sitting in a nature poem.
"I leapt blind into darkness and found sight,"
he thought, and grew all quivery with delight.
He reveled so in his creative discovery,

thrilled, amazed, overcome and shivery,
his feelings were so genuine and visceral,
his long ears tingled and his whiskers bristled.
So taken was he with his paradox,
he quite failed to notice the red fox,
the reason he'd been frantic in the first place
(the fox had come on him and given chase).
But that pre-dated his illumination,
his leap into the dark and liberation.
The fox was the furthest thing from his mind,
so he was startled but not displeased to find
the Red One looking into his gentle eyes.
"After all, a poem's ending should surprise,"
he thought. "And, anyway, life is short and art —"
The fox then drove the truth home to his heart.

Jim Wayne Miller

MEETING

My shadow was my partner in the row.
He was working the slick-handled shadow of his hoe
when out of the patch toward noon there came the sound
of steel on steel two inches underground—
as if our hoes had hooked each other on that spot.
My shadow's hoe must be of steel, I thought.
And where my chopping hoe came down and struck,
memory rushed like water out of rock.
"When two strike hoes," I said, "it's always sign
they'll work the patch together again sometime.
An old man told me that the last time ever
we worked this patch and our hoes rang together."
Delving there with my hoe, I half-uncovered
a plowpoint, worn and rusted over.
"The man I hoed with last lies under earth,
his plowpoint and his saying of equal worth."
My shadow, standing by me in the row,
waited, and while I rested, raised his hoe.

Maureen Morehead

CHAD

when the little boy

with eyes full of sparrows

died

I threw away my bells
and let my candles burn to
nothing

and imagined
the drunk driver
sitting in a silo
sucking his thumb

but the little boy

with bones light as hay

offers his blanket
to the man
in the silo
and whistles the air
in red backyard
swings

and the little boy

with tapers for fingers

is lighting my bones.

Maureen Morehead

TEACHING CHILDREN

is becoming
a psychiatrist
in the bathroom
        a friend of turtles
        eating sweet potato plants
            a kisser of sores
god and the devil
in one

teaching children is tearing your soul
        into a thousand jagged
            bloody pieces and
throwing them all but
one
into a green
garbage can

that one
you push into
your flowered bra
        and keep for a
            band-aid.

Maureen Morehead

THE PURPLE LADY AND BIRTH

One time
the purple lady
curled herself tightly
into a tuna-fish can
because the world looked like
a large weeping woman
in a red blouse
and she could no longer
think of the trees as her babies.

At that time
the purple lady found death easy:
growing small as a sperm cell,
black as night clutter
and all the caves curled up
inside the earth like dogs.
The purple lady entered
where beautiful women forget their faces,
the lights in the ceiling,
the men who touch
and touching back the men.

Who is to say
what made the difference—
jelly of skin, bone, teeth, smell, God,
the baker sifting his white dust
over the floor
of the cave.
The purple lady unwound her body
and ate the wide air
until she was tall as her mother
leaning toward rain,
slash, fire,
sparkle, breath.

Maureen Morehead

SETTING IT RIGHT

The summer I was nineteen
I met a man
on some steps outside a library.
I was wearing a green skirt
with yellow flowers on it.
He had pianos in his head. I could tell
by the way he taught me
to move closer, from the first, be constant,
to listen,
watch his pretty mouth.

A man who builds things is more like my father.
This man took things torn apart
and wished them back together again.
(When I fell apart,
a defeat as significant as a young woman's
losing her virginity for fear;
walking past the library
I thought, this is some victory)
When I fell apart,
this man came from out of nowhere
and taking something shiny from his pocket
gave virginity back to me.

When a man is a sonata,
there is nothing a woman can do,
but listen. And spread her skirts about her
like a tablecloth, it is such a fine day for a picnic, or
pretending she is a parachute,
invite him in,
and ride.

Lee Pennington

SEGOVIA'S FINGERNAIL

He flings music from strings
like spreading star seeds, fingers
counting galaxies in the quiet dark
of light barely beyond a candle range.

One man, mostly a shadow above a stool,
his foot invading a smaller one velvet red,
a guitar on his lap delicate like robin eggs,
releases stolen seeds which hang star planted
in walls like ancient odors
slipping from an opened lid of forgotten
trunk.

The silence of thousands the deepest of all—
full like the great dark places in space.

Together on the front row, he sits—hands
folded on his lap almost in final pose
without the coins on his eyes, head down
the sounds cover him like a comet's
tail always away from the sun; she
watches all, more than hearing—the
man, guitar, fingers, foot on red velvet;
the thousands still in breath-stopped silence;
her hands stroke the mink wrapped around
shoulders;
her own fingers feel the music of fur.

He doesn't see, but thinks he hears one lost
note,
and sits wondering if such is the same
as words never spoken.

She sees it all, thinking maybe even
the hair-line crack before the strings
ripping—
shooting it like a meteor to the front stage
where it lies shaped like a moon's beginning
dark to full—
the haunting color of unmelting ice.

He thinks now the music will go with him
always,
even to the grave, and even then perhaps
hover over the new mound of earth.

But she, long past the hearing (if ever),
already sees it hanging on the wall
neatly framed with fingered gold
and a tiny brass plate saying,
"Segovia's Fingernail."
She knows she must have it and quietly
prepares
to rush the stage at the concert's end—
feigning madness on the floor.

Lee Pennington

CROATOAN

Staggering from the stink of ships—
Months sailed—loaded with supplies
For those in distance a year,
Now perhaps an eternity or
Something less. Men with packs
On their backs sank each
A record of footprints soon lost
To shifting ocean currents.

The forest dripping at the mouth
Like foamy saliva of mad dogs,
And men set down their packs—
Felt their bodies raise a bit
From not-so-pressured sand.
For a moment, they stood. Later,
After staring into nothingness,
Wiped mist from their faces—
Commented on the nothing again.

Blank-eyed Englishmen dragged
Themselves through the trees,
Gathering saliva on their necks—
Saliva from trees and mad-dog cobwebs.
(Cobwebs too heavy to be gossamers)
Webs destined to be only parasites
On traveling men, curious men.

Lee Pennington

CROSS

ain't
my Dad
that put it
on
us all.

ain't my
Tree
they hung
him on.

ain't I
what skinned
and squeezed
him into a plastic
Jesus.

Lee Pennington

DAWN'S TIME

In the morning hours I've watched time
crawl on dawn's fingers slipping silently
shoving shadows around the marigolds
spreading back stardust turned dew—
tiny gold droplets a birdbath for feather
songs.

Slipping silently on red fingers
delighting sailors, red as waking eyes
rubbing back the grey of spider's breath
and spinning through it all, whirling
down locked in love of ancient
maples.

Fingers become curtains, no drapes,
pulled on a blushing universe whose light
spills through and the nude morning
Salome dances mysterious and hypnotic—
the great red platter on which already my head is
waiting.

Jane Stuart

THE SYSTEM

The nervous ant pretends to be
bent on self preservation.
His stiff blue collar soaked with sweat
he grapples with the ration
of crumbs the wind has blown his way
and what the dew has trapped
in drops beneath prim blades of grass.
His little brain is sapped
with platitudes. It's blind man's bluff—
he saves and stores away.
But if fate stomps him underfoot—
he never lived today!

Jane Stuart

NEW YEAR

Wide tracks yawn beneath
the holly tree
here at the old hotel
where street cars sleep
dreaming linen litanies
of motion.

Like carolers, we wander
up and down
the golden street,
brave christians
with our cheeks turned
to the night,
following
the shadow of
the orphan's candles;
listening
to the tremble of
another year
we have betrayed;
reminiscing
in the warmth of closed shop windows,
sorting out the merchandise
receiving or rejecting or refusing
to believe,
blaming

our each defection
on the loneliness
that we cannot
clock or computerize,
the constant jingle of a memory
that no heart has
the heart to silence,
the bubble of
a dream just born,
the fantasy
of satin bootsteps
falling along
a peaceful path,

beside the silver street car rails,

up and down the golden street,

following
the shadow of
our children's candles.

Jane Stuart

RED RASPBERRIES

You have gone to lie down
between heaven and hell
and left me to rummage alone
through empty barn lofts
where brown mice wind day's clocks
and a hound chews a cabbage-stalk bone.

I would bring you fresh raspberries
rubbed red by the sweat
of my belly bent down in the grass,
if only I knew, as I drag myself through
each hour, which way you will pass.

Jane Stuart

MAENAD

When I am consumed, at last, by my lust,
let the winds filter through my fragile dust,
sifting the soul from the evil interred,
blowing it back, without a word,
to a merciful god who will not remember
the ivory flame that burned with such splendor—
but judge me for what I chose to become:
a chanter of Euhoe, a slave to the sun.

Jesse Stuart

MOUNTAIN FUNERAL

We could not stay about the house
Where so many were crying;
We pushed on through the sobbing crowd
From where the corpse was lying.

We walked the path behind the house
Among his blooming trees
And wondered if he dreamed again
Of gathering fruit from these.

His lank bay mules he used for plowing
The sandy upland loam
Played in the barnlot willow-shaded
Behind his mountain home.

His rusty ax stuck in the block.
In the furrow set his plow;
The calloused hands that used them
Were cold and lifeless now.

The bees he loved were working on
The tall wind-waves of clover;
The evening winds he loved to hear
Were softly blowing over.

Jesse Stuart

BLACK APRIL

Only God
Could beat Flint Sycamore
When he played his last trump:
In the loam he battled for bread.

In March
Flint moved to W-Hollow
In a two horse surry,
His wife, Lucy, by his side.

He drove
A white horse with black feet,
A black horse with white feet,
Until sundown
On a third day.

Flint stopped the horses,
Tied two loose leather reins
To two white pine tree roots;
He sifted pine tree loam
Through his scrawny fingers. . .
"A place to build," he said.

He fed the horses corn
From the two horse surrey,
Tied them a rope's length to graze.
Lucy broiled a ham supper
From a pine cone fire.

They bedded in the open,
In the freedom of space. . .
Only the wind in the pine tops,

The horses' neighs
The lone wolf's howl,
And the caw caws of dreaming crows
In the black tree tops:
These for resonant tones. . .

Morning.
Flint pitched a pine pole house,
A wind structure
Daring a pavilion of wind.

He unbeveled his ax
From an emory piece,
Fell trees for corn space.
Lucy daubed the pine pole house
With mud and sticks
Against the wind and tomorrow.

Flint Sycamore planted April corn:
In the loam he battled for bread.
Spring was late; April, black. . .
Corn rotted in the ground;
Potatoes lay under dogwood surf;
Cane never sprouted at all. . .

The crows sang caw caws to the wind
And to each other. . .
They built nests of pine pole limbs
And daubed the cracks with mud and sticks.
The crows laughed
And the winds sang. . .

Flint Sycamore said:
"God, I'll beat you yet."
His first born came
A mangled mass
Of amalgamated
Blood and dust. . .

The crows laughed and sang
To the wind and to each other;
For they too had built a house.

The horses ate
An incredible variety of plants,
Took the murrain,
Were left a stench upon the wind.

Black April. . .

Flint staggered back:
"God, I'll beat you yet."
God beat Flint Sycamore.
His marshland fever
Cut Flint down
Like a weed in autumn.

Down in a meadow
Where two dim lettered
Lichen sandstones
Are marveled at by
Long gray lines of
Traffic comers, goers;
Sleeps Flint Sycamore.

* * * * * * *

Twelve men,
Are sitting at a picnic table
White clothed
With rarest food.
Life is a pleasure they say,
And God is kind.

They look at the green meadow
And the dim lettered lichen stones
Shaded by a tall grass of undying beauty:
Shaded with a wild cherry
With a thousand white sprays

Daring the wind. . .
Life from the richest earth;
Life from a daring dust;
April life from the bosom
Of Flint Sycamore.

Jesse Stuart

HOLD APRIL

Hold on to April; never let her pass!
Another year before she comes again
To bring us wind as clean as polished glass
And apple blossoms in soft, silver rain.
Hold April when there's music in the air,
When life is resurrected like a dream,
When wild birds sing up flights of windy stair
And bees love alder blossoms by the stream.
Hold April's face close yours and look afar;
Hold April in your arms in dear romance.
While holding her look to the sun and star
And with her in her faerie dreamland dance.
Do not let April go but hold her tight,
Month of eternal beauty and delight.

Jesse Stuart

BE KIND TO DUST

Be kind to grains of dust that sting your face
For senseless winds have no thoughts of tomorrow;
Later they might deposit you someplace,
Yesterday's lips that kissed with joy and sorrow.

Remember, you are made of what you curse,
Those particles now getting in your eyes;
And getting in your mouth you think is worse,
Those little flecks of dust you so despise.

Who knows what brains and hearts these once have been?
And through what arteries these once have flowed?
Pumped by strong hearts of women and of men?
And by their love's emotions, paced and slowed?

Be kind to dust but curse the senseless wind
If foolishly you must waste your emotion;
Remember, living dust will in the end
Lose love and beauty, duty, and devotion.

Hollis Summers

BRIDGE FREEZES BEFORE ROAD SURFACE

All of the Commencement speakers were right, Alice:
Life is a treadmill from Albany
At least as far as Syracuse and possibly
Farther and further. But there's no good in being

Despondent, Alice. You can make your way
Almost asleep through the identical miles
From Rest Stop to Rest Stop smiling
To smile at the identical waitress who serves

A single meal. Just because you've seen one
Doesn't mean you shouldn't smile again
At the carbon copied service station man
Serving his single fuel. Be comfortable

Knowing the exact location of lavatory,
Soap, and toilet, as well as where to purchase
Your anniversary cup and a joke in a package.
After all, you do not move singly, Alice.

Hollis Summers

FIGURE

A few paintings remember Joseph.
He helps in the composition,
Making a kind of trinity.

I've seen his figure
At the end of a hospital corridor
Smelling of ether.

A few churches remember him—
One in Sicily;
There's a festival, or two, or three.

But he was around through all the story.
He was probably tired and old.
He took a long trip.

He probably warmed the child's clothes
At a fire made of brambles;
He probably sang to the child.

I know he held the child.
I would remember him a father,
If foster, tending.

Hollis Summers

MANUAL FOR THE FREEWAY

When passing another car
Do not look at the other driver.
When being overtaken
Do not look at the other driver.

Motorists use
Freeways
For being
Alone.

Should you catch other eyes
Pretend you do not see.
Should other eyes see you see
Do not smile or nod.

Should you smile
The other driver
Assumes
You ridicule.

Should you nod
The other driver must run you down.

Where else can a person go to cry?
Where else can a person go?

Hollis Summers

TUNNEL

Tunnel, Slow,
The sign says to the two of us
Who have traveled long together,
Remove Sun Glasses,
Reduce Speed,
Turn Lights on Low,
Stay in Lane;
The world is full of signs
For married people;
And we are used to tunnels,
Faint walls and ceilings,
Funeral parlor light;
We are customed to obey.

But I remember a curve of light
Promising other tunnels' ends,
And always before,
If I remember rightly,
We have followed other cars,
Overtaking the red eyes
Of sudden leaders;
There must be a curve
Within this tunnel;
The tunnel probably ends;
We must drive alone together
Even if no sign says
Tunnel Ends.

Allen Tate

THE WOLVES

There are wolves in the next room waiting
With heads bent low, thrust out, breathing
At nothing in the dark; between them and me
A white door patched with light from the hall
Where it seems never (so still is the house)
A man has walked from the front door to the stair.
It has all been forever. Beasts claw the floor.
I have brooded on angels and archfiends
But no man has ever sat where the next room's
Crowded with wolves, and for the honor of man
I affirm that never have I before. Now while
I have looked for the evening star at a cold window
And whistled when Arcturus spilt his light,
I've heard the wolves scuffle, and said: So this
Is man; so—what better conclusion is there—
The day will not follow night, and the heart
Of man has a little dignity, but less patience
Than a wolf's, and a duller sense that cannot
Smell its own mortality. (This and other
Meditations will be suited to other times
After dog silence howls his epitaph)
Now remember courage, go to the door,
Open it and see whether coiled on the bed
Or cringing by the wall, a savage beast
Maybe with golden hair, with deep eyes
Like a bearded spider on a sunlit floor,
Will snarl—and man can never be alone.

Allen Tate

THE SWIMMERS

Scene: Montgomery County,
        Kentucky, July 1911

Kentucky water, clear springs: a boy fleeing
  To water under the dry Kentucky sun,
  His four little friends in tandem with him, seeing

Long shadows of grapevine wriggle and run
  Over the green swirl; mullein under the ear
  Soft as Nausicaa's palm; sullen fun

Savage as childhood's thin harmonious tear:
  O fountain, bosom source undying-dead
  Replenish me the spring of love and fear

And give me back the eye that looked and fled
  When a thrush idling in the tulip tree
  Unwound the cold dream of the copperhead.

—Along the creek and road was winding; we
  Felt the quicksilver sky. I see again
  The shrill companions of that odyssey:

Bill Eaton, Charlie Watson, "Nigger" Layne
  The doctor's son, Harry Duesler who played
  The flute: and Tate, with water on the brain.

Dog-days: the dusty leaves where rain delayed
Hung low on poison-oak and scuppernong,
And we were following the active shade

Of water, that bells and bickers all night long.
"No more'n a mile," Layne said. All five stood still.
Listening, I heard what seemed at first a song;

Peering, I heard the hooves come down the hill.
The posse passed, twelve horse; the leader's face
Was worn as limestone on an ancient sill.

Then, as sleepwalkers shift from a hard place
In bed, and rising to keep a formal pledge
Descend a ladder into empty space.

We scuttled down the back below a ledge
And marched stiff-legged in our common fright
Along a hog-track by the riffle's edge:

Into a world where sound shaded the sight
Dropped the dull hooves again; the horsemen came
Again, all but the leader. It was night

Momently and I feared: eleven same
Jesus-Christers unmembered and unmade,
Whose Corpse had died again in dirty shame.

The bank then levelling in a speckled glade,
We stopped to breathe above the swimming hole;
I gazed at its reticulated shade

Recoiling in blue fear, and felt it roll
Over my ears and eyes and lift my hair
Like seaweed tossing on a sunk atoll.

I rose again. Borne on the copper air
A distant voice green as a funeral wreath
Against a grave: "That dead nigger there."

The melancholy sheriff slouched beneath
A giant sycamore; shaking his head
He plucked a sassafras twig and picked his teeth:

"We come too late." He spoke to the tired dead
Whose ragged shirt soaked up the viscous flow
Of blood in which It lay discomfited.

A butting horse-fly gave one ear a blow
And glanced off, as the sheriff kicked the rope
Loose from the neck and hooked it with his toe

Away from the blood.—I looked back down the slope:
The friends were gone that I had hoped to greet.—
A single horseman came at a slow lope

And pulled up at the hanged man's horny feet;
The sheriff noosed the feet, the other end
The stranger tied to his pommel in a neat

Slip-knot. I saw the Negro's body bend
And straighten, as a fish-line cast transverse
Yields to the current that it must subtend.

The sheriff's Goddamn was a murmured curse
Not for the dead but for the blinding dust
That boxed the cortege in a cloudy hearse

And dragged it towards our town. I knew I must
Not stay till twilight in that silent road;
Sliding my bare feet into the warm crust,

I hopped the stonecrop like a panting toad
Mouth open, following the heaving cloud
That floated to the court-house square its load

Of limber corpse that took the sun for shroud.
There were three figures in the dying sun
Whose light were company where three was crowd.

My breath crackled the dead air like a shotgun
As, sheriff and the stranger disappearing,
The faceless head lay still. I could not run

Or walk, but stood. Alone in the public clearing
This private thing was owned by all the town,
Though never claimed by us within my hearing.

Allen Tate

SONNETS AT CHRISTMAS 1934

I

This is the day His hour of life draws near,
Let me get ready from head to foot for it
Most handily with eyes to pick the year
For small feed to reward a feathered wit.
Some men would see it an epiphany
At ease, at food and drink, others at chase
Yet I, stung lassitude, with ecstacy
Unspent argue with the season's difficult case
So: Man, dull critter of enormous head,
What would he look at in the coiling sky?
But I must kneel unto the Dead
While Christmas bells of paper white and red,
Figured with boys and girls spilt from a sled,
Ring out the slience I am nourished by.

II

Ah, Christ, I love you rings to the wild sky
And I must think a little of the past:
When I was ten I told a stinking lie
That got a black boy whipped; but now at last
The going years, caught in an accurate glow,
Reverse like balls englished upon green baize—
Let them return, let the round trumpets blow
The ancient crackle of the Christ's deep gaze.
Deafened and blind, with senses yet unfound,
Am I, untutored to the after-wit
Of knowledge, knowing a nightmare has no
  sound;
Therefore with idle hands and head I sit
In late December before the fire's daze
Punished by crimes of which I would be quit.

Robert Penn Warren

MAD YOUNG ARISTOCRAT ON BEACH

He sits in blue trunks on the sand, and children sing.
Their voices are crystal and sad, and tinkle in sunlight.
Their voices are crystal, and the tinkling
Of sadness, like gold ants, crawls on his quivering heart in its midnight.
And the sea won't be still, won't be still,
In that freaking and fracture and dazzle of light.
Yes, somebody ought to take steps and stop it.
It's high time that somebody did, and he thinks that he will.
Why, it's simple, it's simple, just get a big mop and mop it,
Till it's dry as a bone—you sea, you *cretino*, be still!
But he's tired, he is tired, and wants only sleep.
Oh, Lord, let us pray that the children stop singing before he begins to
weep.

If he wept, we just couldn't bear it, but look, he is smiling!
He ponders how charming it is to smile, and magnanimous.
And his smile, indeed, is both sweet and beguiling,
And joy floods his heart now like hope, to replace that old dark animus.
So look! at the great concert grand,
He is bowing, and bowing, and smiling now on us,
And smiles at the sea, at the sea's bright applause—
But fame, ah, how sad! Again he sits on the sand,
And thinks how all human rewards are but gauds and gewgaws,
And lets sand, grain by grain, like history slip from his hand.
But his mother once said that his smile was sweet.
Curse the bitch, it is power man wants, and like a black cloud now mount
to his feet

He is young and sun-brown and tall and well formed, and he knows it.
He will swim in the sea, the water will break to his will.
Now emerging on shore, he is lethal, he shows it.
Yes, let them beware that brute jaw-jut and eye cold now and still.
And let him beware, beware—
That brother, the elder, who comes to the title.
But a title, *merde!* he will marry a passport,
And dollars, of course—he has blood, though he isn't the heir.
Then sudden as death, a thought stops him chillingly short:
Mais l'Amerique, merde! why it's full of Americans there.
So closes his eyes, longs for home, longs for bed.
Ah, that sweet-haunched new housemaid! But knows he can't get her
except in the dark of his head.

So thinks of a whore he once had: she was dull as a sow,
And not once, never once, showed affection. He thinks he will cry.
Then thinks, with heart sweet, he'll be dead soon now,
And opens his eyes to the blaze and enormousness of the sky.
And we watch him, we watch him, and we
Are lonely, are lonely as death, though we try
To love him, but can't, for we sit on the sand,
And eyes throb at the merciless brilliance and bicker of sea,
While sand, grain by grain, like our history, slips from his hand.
We should love him, because his flesh suffers for you and for me,
As our own flesh should suffer for him, and for all
Who will never come to the title, and be loved for themselves, at
innocent nightfall.

Robert Penn Warren

LATE SUBTERFUGE

The year dulls toward its eaves—dripping end.
We have kept honor yet, or lost a friend;
Observed at length the inherited defect;

Known error's pang—but then, what man is perfect?
The grackles, yellow-beaked, beak-southward, fly
To the ruined ricelands south, leaving empty our sky.

This year was time for decision to be made.
No time to waste, we said, and so we said:
This year is time. Our grief can be endured,
For we, at least, are men, being inured
To wrath, to the unjust act, if need, to blood;
And we have faith that from evil may bloom good.

Our feet in the sopping woods will make no sound,
The winter's rot begun, the fox in ground,
The snake cold-coiled, secret in cane the weasel.
In pairs we walk, heads bowed to the long drizzle—
With women some, and take their rain-cold kiss;
We say to ourselves we learn some strength from this.

Robert Penn Warren

DRAGON COUNTRY: TO JACOB BOEHME

This is the dragon's country, and these his own streams.
The slime on the railroad rails is where he has crossed the track.
On a frosty morning, that field mist is where his great turd steams,
And there are those who have gone forth and not come back.

I was only a boy when Jack Simms reported the first depredation,
What something had done to his hog pen. They called him a God-damn liar.
Then said it must be a bear, after some had viewed the location,
With fence rails, like matchwood, splintered, and earth a bloody mire.

But no bear had been seen in the county in fifty years, they knew.
It was something to say, merely that, for people compelled to explain
What, standing in natural daylight, they couldn't believe to be true;
And saying the words, one felt in the chest a constrictive pain.

At least, some admitted this later, when things had got to the worst—
When, for instance, they found in the woods the wagon turned on its side,
Mules torn from trace chains, and you saw how the harness had burst.
Spectators averted the face from the spot where the teamster had died.

But that was long back, in my youth, just the first of case after case.
The great hunts fizzled. You followed the track of disrepair,
Ruined fence, blood-smear, brush broken, but came in the end to a place
With weed unbent and leaf calm—and nothing, nothing, was there.

So what, in God's name, could men think when they couldn't bring to bay
That belly-dragging earth-evil, but found that it took to air?
Thirty-thirty or buckshot might fail, but then at least you could say
You had faced it—assuming, of course, that you had survived the affair.

We were promised troops, the Guard, but the Governor's skin got thin
When up in New York the papers called him Saint George of Kentucky.
Yes, even the Louisville reporters who came to Todd County would grin.
Reporters, though rarely, still come. No one talks. They think it unlucky.

If a man disappears—well, the fact is something to hide.
The family says, gone to Akron, or up to Ford, in Detroit.
When we found Jebb Johnson's boot, with the leg, what was left, inside,
His mother said, no, it's not his. So we took it out to destroy it.

Land values are falling, no longer do lovers in moonlight go.
The rabbit, thoughtless of air gun, in the nearest pasture cavorts.
Now certain fields go untended, the local birth rate goes low.
The coon dips his little black paw in the riffle where he nightly resorts.

Yes, other sections have problems somewhat different from ours.
Their crops may fail, bank rates rise, loans at rumor of war be called,
But we feel removed from maneuvers of Russia, or other great powers,
And from much ordinary hope we are now disenthralled.

Robert Penn Warren

THE CHILD NEXT DOOR

The child next door is defective because the mother,
Seven brats already in that purlieu of dirt,
Took a pill, or did something to herself she thought would not hurt,
But it did, and no good, for there came this monstrous other.

The sister is twelve. Is beautiful like a saint.
Sits with the monster all day, with pure love, calm eyes.
Has taught it a trick, to make *ciao*, Italian-wise.
It crooks hand in that greeting. She smiles her smile without taint.

I come, and her triptych beauty and joy stir hate
—Is it hate?—in my heart. Fool, doesn't she know that the process
Is not that joyous or simple, to bless, or unbless,
The malfeasance of nature or the filth of fate?

Can it bind or loose, that beauty in that kind,
Beauty of benediction? We must trust our hope to prevail
That heart-joy in beauty be wisdom, before beauty fail
And be gathered like air in the ruck of the world's wind!

I think of your goldness, of joy, but how empires grind, stars are hurled
I smile stiff, saying *ciao*, saying *ciao*, and think: *This is the world.*

PLAYS

Wendell Berry

THE BRINGER OF WATER

The people in the play:

Mat Feltner
A farmer of the town of Port William, Kentucky. He is now sixty-five years old.

Margaret Feltner
Mat's wife, about sixty-three.

Hannah Feltner
The widow of Virgil, the son of Mat and Margaret, killed in the final spring of World War II.

Little Margaret
Daughter of Virgil and Hannah Feltner. She is three years old.

Henry Catlett
Son of Mat's and Margaret's daughter.

Old Jack Beechum
Mat's uncle, a farmer, now eighty-four years old, living in town.

An old man, an old woman, a young woman
Neighbors of the Feltners.

Burley and Jarrat Coulter
Brothers. Farmers. Burley is fifty-three, Jarrat fifty-eight.

Nathan Coulter
Jarrat's son, twenty-four years old, a veteran of the war.

SCENE 1

The Feltner's back porch in early July, 1948. It is after the noon meal, for Mat a moment of deliberate ease before the afternoon's work in the field. Mat and Margaret sit together on the porch. Though their chairs are rocking chairs, they sit still. An earthen jug of water stands at Mat's feet. Hannah sits in a swing hung from the limb of a shade tree out in the yard. Sewing, she looks up from time to time to watch her daughter and Henry Catlett, who sits on the grass near her. To amuse the little girl Henry is building a house of brightly colored blocks.

Margaret: She worries me. Three years
now since Virgil was killed
in the war, and still she keeps
to herself, saying nothing
of what she's concerned with most.

Mat: If it wasn't for the children
—and Uncle Jack, whatever
company he is to her—
she might as well be alone.
She troubles me too.
I'd like to see her happy.
But mostly I'd like to see her
turn back to the world
and take up life again
for what it's worth.
That she seems so fearful
is what worries me.

Margaret: Well, I know the fear
of change, how time passing
threatens her with the worst
she can think of. The past
taints the future. Sometimes
so much is lost in it
that only enough seems left
to grieve and to be afraid.
But you're right. The fear
of nothing in particular
is a waste.

Mat: I reckon after all
it's lucky she has the child.

Margaret: It's not in her children
that a woman can live. Not
in the future. She lives
in living with her man
who is the present, asking,
changing, filling hand
and heart, not with the hoped
or the mourned, but with his life
as it is, what is possible in time.

Mat: Maybe so. A nice thing anyhow,
mam, for a lady to say
to her husband. It may be
a change will come. I've noticed
Nathan Coulter looking at her
when she brings water to the field
or he comes by the house.
It's not the look, I'd say,
of a lover who has been at all
encouraged, but it's a look
I understand.

Margaret: And it's a look
that Hannah understands,
don't doubt it—and even
values, as a young woman has to.
But that it moves her warns her
to hold herself away,
and she treats him with a cold
politeness women have, that won't
speak until it has to.

They sit in silence a moment. And then Mat stands up stiffly, a little wearily.

Mat: Oh me! I reckon I'd better
be getting on back.
They'll already be there.

He picks up his jug and starts across the back yard toward a little slatted gate. Hannah looks up at him as he passes, smiling at him.

Hannah: I'm sorry you have to go
back out there. It's so hot.

Mat: Yes. It' hot. It's beating down.

Hannah: You'll be needing water
later?

Mat: About three o'clock,
I expect. A fresh drink then
would help us last till night.

He goes on across the yard and through the gate. The others watch him go.

SCENE 2

Hannah, accompanied by Henry and Old Jack, is on the way to the field to take water to the men at work there. Generally, Henry goes in front of Hannah, adventuring, calling back. Old Jack comes last, usually too far behind to talk to the others. From time to time, glancing back, Hannah stops to let the old man rest, though to spare his feelings she always makes it appear that she wants to rest. At the beginning they come up to and pass a man and two women picking pole beans in a neighboring garden.

Hannah: I became the vessel of all
of him that could live,
his seed's earth. I held
still as if balanced
in a light little boat, for fear
I'd hurt the last chance
his life had to be alive.
Then little Margaret was born.
There could be no other
like her, and still I kept
still, thinking all the time
of her. And now she's growing,
not a baby any more.
At times I see her draw away
from me toward the others,

and I know her life
is hers, and mine is mine.
I begin to feel again
the claims on me my life has.
As though I felt my body
touched in the night, I want
to be talked to, touched,
for only my own sake.

The old woman: Here she comes with her bucket
again, with the little Catlett boy
and that scandalous old man
Jack Beechum, them two
she trusts herself to. I'd say
she's a strange one, with her looks
and all, living like a nun.

The old man: Nuns, they say, is married
to Jesus.

The old woman: That might be.
And then again it mightn't.
That one there is married
to a dead man, and there ain't
but mighty little future in that.

The young woman *(lowering her voice as Henry passes and Hannah approaches):*
I declare, I'd let those men
carry their own water, if it was me.

The old woman: Maybe that ain't water
to drink. Maybe that's water
to fish in.

The old man: Now Marthy!

Hannah: Good afternoon.

All three: Evening.

Hannah: Picking beans?

The old woman: What the bugs
has left us.

Hannah passes on by.

I said to myself
when Mat and them's boy got killed
in the war, and she was left
to have and raise that baby
by herself, I said it's a pity
they don't think beforehand,
before they go to marrying
and begetting and visiting
the Lord God only knows what
on some poor innocent thing
that never caused none of it.

Hannah: Like a baking or a pregnancy
the time has come to fullness
and can be no fuller.
It can't go on being
what it is. I haven't tried
to change it, but I feel
it changing. I feel it
in the air, hovering over me
and all I'm part of,
like the closeness before the rain.

Henry: Hannah, come look!

He examines what he has picked up from the path, then puts it in his pocket, and again searches the ground.

Hannah: I'm coming.

Old Jack: There's a cloud in the west
and with it so hot and still
it ought to rain. I'm dry,
an old man with his death
coming. The thought of a grave
with the grass green on it
and the rain wetting it
seems bearable to me now.
Seems good. The only youth
I'll have again is in it.

The old man: Evening, Jack!

Old Jack: Evening
to you!

The old man: Mighty hot, I'd say,
for two old birds like us
to be out in the sun, stirring.
We ought to be in the shade
somewhere, setting and resting.

Old Jack: Setting and resting, hell!
Setting and resting'll soon
make a dead man out of you.
A man like myself, with only
twenty or thirty more years
to live, has got to be *rattling*.

The old woman: Huh! Well, it's a coming.
And you'd better be right
with your maker when it comes.

Old Jack: Well, a man has to hope
he'll somehow be overlooked.

The old woman: Jack Beechum, it don't make
no difference how much
land you got nor how much
money you got nor who you are,
death's a coming to you.
It don't miss a one.

Old Jack: Death's very democratic.
I've heard it. Maybe it is.

The old man *(indulgently correcting):*
Jack, Marthy ain't no democrat.

Old Jack is already going on.

The young woman: Poor old feller. Look at him.
He *ain't* got long to be around.
He can't hardly make it.

Old Jack: Piss on them! They'd like
to cover up a hard fact
by dripping pity on it.
Molasses on bad bread.
They think a man is bound
to die mourning, clamped
to the world like a trap.
They'd have me quaver and bleat,
leaving this place,
as though I didn't know
what it's cost me. They think
I'm childish, or a child.
I'm an old man, and I
know where I've been.
The churchly ones are worst.
They'd have me glad to go.
The world's cursed, they say,
and to trade it off
for Heaven and Heaven's grace
is an everlasting bargain.
It's a gamble, I say,
and for better and worse
I like this place.
The world's curse is a man
who'd rather be someplace else.

He stops to rest, and up ahead, noticing, Hannah stops also.

The walking tires me out.
I'll have to quit this.
But there's the field there
and the men at work. I want
to know what they have to say
and how the crop is.

Henry *(Running back down the path to Hannah):*
I found an arrowhead! I never
found one before. Look at it.
I found it right in the path
where people wore away the dirt
over it, walking on it.
Hannah, look!

Hannah: I'm looking.

Henry: Well, why don't you like it?

Hannah: I do. I do. It's nice.

Henry: How do you reckon it got there?
Do you reckon he shot at something
and missed?

Hannah: Maybe he lost it.

Henry: Maybe he killed something.
Do you reckon? Maybe he killed
some*body* with it. In a war.

Hannah: I hope not.

Henry: Why?

Hannah: I want
things to live. I want things
that have lived to have lived,
and things that are living
to stay alive. And I hope
things that might live *will* live.

Henry *(to Old Jack, who has rested and is coming on again):*
Look, Uncle Jack, what I found.
An arrowhead. How do you
reckon it got here?

Old Jack: Ay Lord, honey,
this ground's a lot older
than anything I know.

They go on together a little way, and Hannah stops at a walled spring and fills her bucket. She offers the dipper to Old Jack.

Hannah: Drink. While it's fresh.

Old Jack *(drinks and puts the dipper back in the bucket):*
That's good. That spring never
has gone dry in my time,
though I've seen it dwindle
mighty small once or twice.
I stopped and drank here
when I was a boy, younger
than this boy, and my daddy
before me stopped and drank
here, and his daddy before him.

Moved by his thoughts, he turns away from them and goes on ahead by himself.

A long time back that spring
was flowing, cool in the summer,
in winter too warm to freeze,
pooled still and clear
where the water catches and brims
on the rock. While we've worked
and taken pleasure and suffered
and died here, it has flowed
like the sound and the feel
and the taste of what this ground
has been to us—kinder to us,
mostly, than we've been to it.
It has been the turning toward us
of the womankindness of the earth.

SCENE 3

The procession arrives at the field's edge, Hannah first with the water bucket, and then Old Jack and Henry. Burley and Jarrat Coulter and Jarrat's son Nathan are with Mat, hoeing the tobacco. They reach the row ends as Hannah comes in sight, and Jarrat draws a file from his pocket and begins sharpening his hoe. As the scene goes on the file is passed from one to another until all four have used it.

Burley: Lord, Lord, look a yonder.
Here comes that water,
and me so dry
I could spit a ball of cotton
from here to town.

He moves into the shade of a tree a little way up the fence, taking his hat off and fanning himself with it as he goes.

And hot! Lord, and the sun
done stopped dead still
up there. I *swear* it ain't
moved an inch the last hour

The other men follow him into the shade. It is clear from the way they move that the coming of the water is an established occasion for rest.

Wilted like a picked rose!
That's me. Give a dying man
a little drop to drink, mam.

Enjoying Burley's gab, which is clearly of a sort she has heard from him before and which is at least partly for her benefit, Hannah brings him the bucket and he lifts the dipper and drinks.

My *my!* That's mighty fine!
I'm glad I lived to drink that.
When the good Lord made
spring water He surely did
have a poor hot tired man
in mind. When He made
spring water He was doing
pret near as good as He did
when He made hot biscuits
and ham and roasting ears
and blackberry cobbler and iced tea.

He looks suddenly at Old Jack, gesturing broadly with the dipper.

"Oh that one would give me a drink
of the water of the well of Beth-lehem,
which is by the gate!"
How bout it, uncle?
Am I telling it right?

Old Jack: Mighty right!

Burley: And Mat,
my friend, am I telling it
right?

Mat: You're telling it right.

Burley *(turns, arms outstretched, hat in one hand, dipper in the other):*

Nathan? My boy? Ain't I
telling it right?

Nathan: Right!

Burley: And Jarrat there, a man
who is serious about work,
and don't believe in speeches
about anything good, he
knows I'm telling it right.
Yes!

He puts the dipper back in the bucket.

So pass on, mam,
and water these folks.

Henry is showing Mat and Jarrat his arrowhead, and Burley goes over to look. Hannah passes among them with the water and they drink, thanking her. She comes last to Nathan, who has remained to the side. He drinks and puts the dipper back. The talk that follows is level and open. They are a man and woman fully experienced, and are neither shy nor coy.

Nathan: I'd like to talk to you.

Hannah: What about?

Nathan: About what
we might mean or be
to each other. Or what we
already are to each other,
I ought to say. All it needs
is talking about. You know it.

Hannah: I do. But setting free
what is from what has been
is another thing. Maybe
it can't be done now,
I've been bound so long
to what's gone by. To live
now, to really live
and hope and take pleasure
for myself, I'd almost have
to come back from the dead.
You ought not to stir things up
that are better left alone.
You ought to let us be
at peace. To get free
of the past I'd have
to bear it all again.
One time was enough.

Nathan: It's already happening to you
or you wouldn't have said that.
You ought to let me come
to see you, take you places.

Hannah: You mean let you call for me
like a beau, and take me out
to supper or a show or someplace
like that. No. Not there
in that house. You understand,
don't you? Somehow I can't
stand the thought of that.

Nathan: Maybe I understand. Maybe I think
you can stand more than you think.
Well, meet me yonder on the hill.

Hannah: When?

Nathan: After supper. Tonight.

Hannah: I won't say I will. I don't . . .

Nathan grins at her.

I know what you're thinking
I haven't said I won't. I don't
know what to think, much less say.
When I asked you when just now
things changed. Wait. We'll see.

Nathan: What's he got?

Hannah: Henry?
He found an arrowhead.
You'd think he found a whole
Indian tribe with lodges
and fires and cornfields.

Nathan: An arrowhead is pretty exciting
for a boy to find. I used
to find them myself when I
was a boy. And they did
almost make me see
the Indians who used to hunt
and raise their crops here.
Boys find arrowheads. Men
are usually looking for something else.

Hannah: I don't like it. I'm sure
it's silly not to, but I don't.
It's a weapon, what men
seem always to have been best at.
I want to let things live.

Nathan: By that very wish, Hannah,
you're in for all the fierceness
and violence life has.
The goodness too. But you can't
escape life by loving it.

He laughs as if both commending and disparaging the neatness of his point. Hannah stands silent.

Burley: Uncle Jack and Mat,
you remember when French Chin
worked for Pap, when Jarrat

and me was boys, and how
tongue-tied he was. French said
he got awful drunk one night
and Pap worked him hard
all day the next day, and old French
said his head was hurting
and it felt so big and heavy
that every time he leaned over
it nearly pulled him to the ground,
and he said, "The sun got about a
h-hour high, and just hu-ung there"

SCENE 4

A sloping field, the top of a high ridge, not far from Mat Feltner's farm. Below, the steeper part of the slope is heavily timbered. The soil worn thin, the field has for some time been abandoned. Now young cedars the height of a man stand on it, scattered twenty or so feet apart, and the ground between them is covered thigh-deep with the lavishly blooming flowers of early July: bee balm, black-eyed Susans, Queen Anne's lace, butterfly weed. Hannah is walking up, alone, to the top of the rise. It is dusk. By the end of the scene it will have darkened until there will be no light left at all.

Hannah: If I didn't want to go
I shouldn't have asked him when.
I knew that, yet I asked.
Uncle Jack would say I'm going
because I want to. I am.
And I'm afraid to go. I feel
the way closing off behind me
as though in every track
my foot leaves in the path
a tree springs up, or a rock
too heavy to move. And I feel
the heavy beauty and grief
of what is past, as though
I'm about to go free of it
by some great pain of birth

and death. I remember a time
not long ago when I'd have cried,
feeling what I feel now,
and been unable to go on.
I know I'll never cry
more tears of that kind.
I'm up now to where I can see
all the town. It's quiet.
The lights are coming on.
The bats are filling the sky
full of their journeywork,
and I hear a screech owl
crying. Where I'm going
I've hardly begun to go.

She walks on a few steps in silence, and then she sees Nathan waiting among the little trees, still as one of them. She merely stops. They are perhaps ten feet apart, and to the end of the scene they don't come any nearer each other.

Nathan: I believed you'd come,
but I'm as glad as if
I'd doubted it.

Hannah: I'm here.
But be slow to understand
what I may mean by it.
I'm not sure myself, yet.

Nathan: I'm middling polite, and tired,
not apt to be in a hurry.

He laughs as he did earlier, as though he can't resist needling her and yet is afraid it will be taken more to heart than he intends. After a moment he seems to turn away from that subject altogether. He turns slightly away from her and stands looking over the field for a time before he speaks again.

I bought this old farm
last week. Did you know that?

Hannah: I heard it.

Nathan *(laughs)*: So did I.
Two weeks before I even
signed the note, I heard
I'd bought it, and paid
three times its worth. That's
Port William. On the alert.
You know what they say?
"Tell a lie and stick to it
long enough, and it'll come true."
That's partly right. Anyhow,
I bought the place. And signed
the note. What do you think of it?

Hannah: Well, it looks awfully grown up
and neglected.

Nathan: You're right.
What else do you think?

Hannah *(hesitates)*:
I wondered why, with Jarrat
and Burley owning land,
you'd want to buy a place.

Nathan: Because I think everybody
ought to have a little
land of his own, or ought
to belong to a little land.
It's part of his manhood,
not to need to ask somebody
where to hang his shovel
or his hat. And sitting around
waiting to inherit a place
is a little bit buzzardish,
wouldn't you say?

Hannah: Yes.
But is this what you wanted?

Nathan: It's not what I wanted.
It's what was here to be had,
and what I could afford.
It's my fate, you could say.

He looks away a moment longer, and then turns back to her.

Look at it. You'd hardly
believe this was virgin ground
not so long ago, and poplars
and white oaks and sugar maples
thicker than two barrels
stood on it, and the soil
was deep and black under them.
That's gone, and here are rocks
and the cedars and the weeds
that love poor land. A place
like this one'll be hard
to live on and take care of,
more work than a better place,
and you know why?
Because for all those years
the people who ought to have
cared for it and done the work
didn't. Do you see
what I mean by fate?
There's a life here for a man
and a woman and family too,
but not as much as there was once.
And a lifetime won't be enough
to bring it back. A man
would have to live maybe
five hundred years
to make it good again
—or learn something of the cost
of not making it good.
But hard as it is, I accept
this fate. I even like it
a little—the idea of making
my lifetime one of the several
it will take to bring back
the possibilities to this place
that used to be here.
And for several evenings now
I've been coming here
and standing and looking,
and I can imagine my life

being lived here—even
the little details of it,
workdays and fencerows and such.
I could say a lot more.

Hannah: I think what you say
is good.

Nathan: Where'd you leave
the baby?

Hannah: With her grandmother,
waiting on the front porch
to see if an owl would hoot.

Nathan: Where do they think you went?

Hannah: For a walk to get cool.

Nathan: You didn't tell them where.

Hannah: Not who I was going to see.

Nathan: You're really on the sly, then.

Hannah: Please, Nathan, don't shame me.

Her voice has become suddenly resonant with feeling, and for a moment they are both quiet, acknowledging this. They seem to realize that, having spoken so, she now stands more open to him. In what she said, in the tone of her voice, their history has begun.

Nathan: No. I won't. I didn't
mean to.

Hannah: Virgil
was their son. They made me
their daughter. They've left
no kindness undone. I have
to think of them.

Nathan: But Hannah,
don't you think they want
you to live your life? I know
they do. I know Mat Feltner,
anyhow, and I know he'd never
put himself ahead of you.

Hannah: No. Neither of them would.
But they hold to what they've
lost, the way we all do.
And I can't turn away from them
as if it didn't matter
or was easy. It does matter,
and it's not easy.

Nathan: It's you.
It's not them. And it's not
what you're turning away from
that worries you. It's what
you're turning toward, all
the unknown you'll face
as soon as you turn toward me.

Hannah: When I turn toward you
it's like the world turning
away from the sun. I only
know what I knew
when I began to turn.

Nathan: And so the question is
is that enough.

Hannah: There's no
chance ever to be touched
in the light. There's only
the dark to be touched in.

Nathan: I know it's an awful risk
I'm asking you to take. I ask,
hoping just that you'll want
to take it, that it'll seem right
to you now—not last week

or next, or in twenty years.
It's not something you'll be able
to figure about, or foresee
any sure happiness in. Clear
as my hope is, I don't know
what's going to happen. The worst
you can think of, maybe.

Hannah: Once,
the worst I could think of
did happen, so I don't doubt
it can. And I can think
of worse things now. I even
fear the worst may be bound
to happen, some destruction
that men will do in crazy hope
or anger or pride—that no man
can either believe or bear.

Nathan: I know. The war has to be
on your mind, bearing proof
of the possibility of wars to come.
The ones of us who went to it
and you who lost by it
will never go free of it.
We can't see to the ground
but by looking through horror.
But fear of the worst may be
the cost of imagining the best.
I think that some, maybe
only a few, a man and woman
here and there, must be willing
to bear the cost of the worst
they foresee, and worse than that,
to allow the best a chance.
They must find the joy to do that,
to be together and live,
or the present's darker than the future.

For maybe half a minute neither says anything. It is full dark now, and there is no sound except for the night insects. And then Nathan says:

Hannah, are you here or gone?
Where are you?

Hannah: Here!

Benjamin Bradford

CONCENTRIC CIRCLES

THE CHARACTERS

ALTHEA PERGANDE — a very old woman

LILLIE PERGANDE — her sister

CLOVIS MITCHELL — a young evangelist

The curtain opens slowly. It is dusk, the lights have not been turned on. Dimly lighted, an interior is seen. There is a large bow window rear center that is raised one step. The furnishings are Edwardian preserved in formalin. There are heavy drapes at the window. To right of the bow is a tall chest. There is a door to an entrance hall, stage right, and a door to the dining room, stage left. Downstage right is a library table heavy with books and old papers. There is a day bed stage left, the head raised a little, with a small table nearby. Near the foot of the day bed is a small chair.

The bow of the window is deep and holds a tall needlepoint screen with an almost completed classical scene. There is a small chair nearby and another small chair at the far left edge of the bow. Right of center downstage is a wheel chair, tall, solid, and wooden. ALTHEA PERGANDE sits quietly in the chair waiting. She wheels herself to the hall door.

ALTHEA: *(Cross and loud)*: Lillie! *(There is no answer.)* What are you doing, Lillie? *(She waits a moment and wheels herself center.)* Dark! *(Disgruntled)* It's pitch dark in here. *(Quietly)* You know how I hate the dark. It's one of your gestures, isn't it, to let it get dark . . . and leave me sitting here in it. *(A door is heard opening and closing.)* Lillie?

LILLIE: *(Wearily)* Yes, Althea. *(She remains off stage a moment.)*

ALTHEA: What are you doing?*(She is exasperated. The day has been long.)*

LILLIE: *(Appearing in the door)* What?

She is a very old woman, dressed in a dark crepe dress hanging loosely to her ankles. The years are heavy on her shoulders. She is two or three years older than ALTHEA.

ALTHEA: *(Louder)* What were you doing? *(ALTHEA keeps her back to LILLIE.)*

LILLIE: *(With no impatience)* You know very well what I was doing. *(She crosses down.)*

ALTHEA: *(With light sarcasm)* It takes an hour to get the paper?

LILLIE: *(Handing her the afternoon paper and crossing left)* I was sitting . . . sitting for a while on the front stoop by the fence watching the sun set on the marigolds.

ALTHEA: *(To the world at large)* Sitting on the stoop, watching the marigolds. And what is Althea doing? Sitting . . . *(Roughly)* in the pitch dark. *(Turning to LILLIE)* I don't expect you to care about that, about me. I've lived long enough with you . . . *alone* . . . to not expect anything more than what I can do for myself which is precious small thanks to you. *(A tirade in crescendo)* You did it to me . . . crippled me . . . *(Turning from her)* Why, I'd be married now, grandchildren all around this house if you hadn't brought me the disease. You brought it home, but it didn't cripple you.

LILLIE has crossed up to the bow window and is peering out the window, oblivious.

You had it, you got up and walked away. *(Scornfully)* But you ruined *my* life, my whole life. *(Turning back to her)* You . . . you're not even listening. *(Wheeling herself to the step of the window)* What are you doing? *(A pause and quietly)* Do you think you're young enough to be free?

LILLIE: *(Turning to her)* No. *(With resignation)* Not young enough to be anything.

ALTHEA: *(Haughtily)* Would you mind turning on the lights? I've spent enough time in darkness. *(Shrinking)* I want to read the obituaries. I want to see who died.

LILLIE crosses to center and pulls the light cord, the stage is filled with a soft light.

The paper's dirty. You know I don't like for the paper to be dirty. Did the boy throw it in the mud or did your shaky old hands drop it there? *(She abruptly wheels back center.)* Sister Lillie, hands aflutter, drops the paper and the butter, drops the eggs and breaks a dozen . . . *(pause)* What rhymes with dozen? *(Casually opening the paper. Unctuously)* Thank goodness the death notices are clean. *(She begins to read.)*

LILLIE: *(Hesitantly)* While I was outside Mrs. Grim walked by. She's older than I am and she was smiling. *(Crossing to the chair at the foot of the day bed.)* What's she got to smile about? *(Sitting)* I haven't smiled in days or months, I don't know which.
Who's gone? *(There is no answer.)* Althea, who's dead we know?

ALTHEA: *(Without looking up)* No one. I don't know a soul listed here. They're all . . . younger. *(A pronouncement)* Funerals: Harry Keith, age sixty-four, 268 Good Sheppard Street, died at 3:30 A.M. *(Looking up)* What a terrible time to die! Imagine dying at 3:30 in the morning. What a bother it must have been. *(Back to the paper)* At home. Survived by his wife, four daughters, son, three sisters and two brothers. Funeral services will be held . . .

LILLIE: Did we know him? *(She is watching ALTHEA intently.)*

ALTHEA: *(Off-handedly)* Of course not. He was of a different generation.

LILLIE: *(With excitement)* Any others?

ALTHEA: *(Blithely)* A page full.

LILLIE: Anyone . . .?

ALTHEA: *(Supercilious, aloof)* No. No one you knew. *(An edge of triumph)* We've outlived them all. William, Genevieve, and Granny Hobson, all dead and down the drain . . . *(Painfully)* And here we sit. *(A pause)* A foolish girl was sister Lillie. Now she's sick, senile, and silly . . . that was an onomatopoeia.

LILLIE: *(Quickly)* Alliteration.

ALTHEA: Onomatopoeia.

LILLIE: *(Almost happy with communication, albeit argumentative)* Alliteration. *(Standing)* I was the teacher, remember? *(One of her few defenses)*

ALTHEA: *(An old battle)* And somehow got the idea that teachers knew everything. Teaching didn't do a thing for your personality, my dear. It made you into a bigot and a bore. *(Superciliously)* Forgive me. You may have been a bore and a bigot before you taught. *(Angrily)* I don't remember, it was so long ago.

LILLIE: *(Firmly)* Would you like the dictionary? I'll bring it to you. *(Moving right to the table)*

ALTHEA: *(Off-handedly)* I've lost interest in figures of speech.

LILLIE: *(Searching about the library table)* I don't think so easily. *(Wanting to hold this level of communication)*

ALTHEA: *(Pouting)* I'd like some water. I'm thirsty.

LILLIE: Wait a minute!

ALTHEA: *(Louder)* I don't want to wait a minute. I'm thirsty. *(Dramatically)* All my life . . . all my life I have waited for minutes . . .

LILLIE: *(Picking up a frayed book)* Here it is. *(A step toward ALTHEA)*

ALTHEA: *(Waving it away)* Put it down and bring me a glass of water.

LILLIE: *(Victory)* Because you know you're wrong. *(Rifling through the A's)* A . . . L . . . L . . .

ALTHEA: *(Crossly)* I have no interest in it.

LILLIE: Here it is. *(Crossing to ALTHEA, putting it before her eyes)* Read it.

ALTHEA: *(Turning her head)* I said I have no interest in it. *(Wheeling a few feet away)* I am interested in my *needs* being met. I am interested in not being constantly irritated by you, by your sense of definition. I am interested in living somewhere in another place with other people. *(Wheeling her chair center)* I am interested in comfort. I am interested in movement . . . clouds on a windy day. I am interested in . . .

LILLIE: I am interested in your acknowledging the fact that you are dead wrong. I want . . .

ALTHEA: I am interested by transfiguration. *(A pause)* The past . . .

LILLIE: Irrevocable!

ALTHEA: Yes, I know. *(Returning to the paper)* And when do I get the water? *(The bravura actress)* I am perishing in a Sahara, ah, an oasis yonder. Seen plainly, not an illusion. And I could have made it, had I not been crippled by my sister at an early age. Piteously looking at my withered limbs . . .*(Her head falls.)* I die . . .

LILLIE replaces the book on the library table and crosses to the dining room door left.

Where are you going?

LILLIE: *(Flatly)* To get the water. *(She exits.)*

ALTHEA: *(Calling after her)* Cold, but not too cold. No ice. Cold enough to frost the glass. *(Calling out)* And I think I'd like the cranberry glass this time. *(Smugly)* I like little changes. *(Reading the paper . . . to herself)* We did know her, but not well . . . great-grandchildren, and so many. Some people multiply like rabbits. No sense of decency. *(Looking up)* Would you hurry? *(Again to herself)* Even proud of it. As if procreation implied sensuality.

LILLIE enters carrying the cranberry glass upon a tray.

LILLIE: *(Apologetically)* It seems . . . *(Offers the tray)*

ALTHEA: *(Drawing herself up, horrified)* There is ice in that water. *(She does not touch it.)*

LILLIE: *(Continuing)* That there is not cold water in the pitcher.

ALTHEA: *(Furious)* You know I hate ice in water. You did it on purpose . . . I won't drink it. I will not drink water with ice in it.

LILLIE: Yesterday you wouldn't . . .

ALTHEA: *(Taunting—bitter)* I do not admire stagnation. I like changes. I told you clearly, concisely that I did not want water with ice. I absolutely will not drink it. *(Again the actress)* I will die before I will touch that water. You may take it back into the kitchen and you may pour it out. *(Wheeling right)* How the privileged punish the unprivileged. . . . *(A brief pause)* I am waiting for an apology. . . . a sign of contrition. . . .

LILLIE crosses up and center, placing the tray upon the chest upstage left.

Is there no contrition? . . . Apparently none.

LILLIE begins to work on the needlepoint.

I could wish that you did not have to help me, service me so to speak. But as you recall, the ability to care for myself was lost a long time ago. *(Airily)* Thanks to you and your disease that hobbled me as a young girl, a pretty, running girl, flaxen hair blowing behind me, running down the streets, around the house . . . never still. Men watched me run. And I watched them watch me run. And you watched them watching me. And for a birthday gift you brought me poliomyelitis. Poliomyelitis. *(Softly)* Poliomyelitis. What a pretty word for shrunken legs that never ran again. *(Sighing)* There's a vaccine now. Little girls running in the streets won't have to beg . . . humble mendicants . . . for a glass of water.

LILLIE: *(Tersely)* I told you I saw Mrs. Grim in the street. She spoke. She said, "hello, Miss Pergande". And I said, "hello, Mrs. Grim".

ALTHEA: What a fascinating thing to hear.

LILLIE: *(Continuing)* She asked me to a revival, a tent revival in that big field at the end of the street.

ALTHEA: *(Still scornful)* Interesting, interesting.

LILLIE: And she smiled, imagine, as old as she is, she smiled. She said the preaching had made her young again. Young in soul.

ALTHEA: No doubt they brought the fountain of youth along.

LILLIE: *(Still working at the needlepoint)* I wanted to go.

ALTHEA: *(Shocked)* You wanted to go?

LILLIE: Yes. *(She looks up.)* I wanted to see what it was about. *(Voice rising)* I wanted something to look forward to.

ALTHEA: You haven't been out of the house except to get my paper in two years.

LILLIE: *(Persistently)* I wanted to go. I wanted to smile again.

ALTHEA: *(Petulant)* What you mean is you wanted to leave me.

LILLIE: *(Lifting her eyes)* To anticipate something. To feel that there is a world outside this house.

ALTHEA: *(Scornfully)* This house *is* the world. My world because I can't go beyond the door. Your world because you made me as I am. *(Turning away from LILLIE)* Why don't you go? *(A sly look)*

LILLIE: *(Carefully)* I'm afraid.

ALTHEA: Of whom, of what? *(Wheeling rapidly back to her)* Of people laughing at your shaky, bony old hands, and your head bobbing side to side? *(Laughing)* You get that here, darling. I laugh at you all the time. *(Bitter)* Of the miracle that won't work for you? *(The actress again)* I envision it. Lillie Pergande, stooped and slow, walking indeed she can walk down the aisle to the miracle of youthful salvation. Young again, indeed. *(Furiously)* Anticipation goes with the color of the hair, the elasticity of the skin. It doesn't come back . . . *(Trailing off)* it never comes back.

LILLIE: *(She affects not to hear most of ALTHEA's words.)* Perhaps that's what I'm afraid of.

ALTHEA: *(Smugly)* Besides I already knew about it. It was in the paper. Near the funeral notices. *(With saccharine)* I'm sorry you can't read the paper this week. You know why! And because of the ice in the water you can't read it next week either.

LILLIE: *(With futility)* Or the week after or the week after or the week after because of dust on a plate, or waking up too late, or reasons too . . .

ALTHEA: *(Strongly)* It is my paper.

LILLIE: I know.

ALTHEA: My paper because I buy it. I have the right to share my things when I wish. I am happy to share with you when you have proved yourself to deserve.

LILLIE: *(Looking at her squarely)* It doesn't matter, Althea, doesn't matter anymore. I just thought again of anticipation.

ALTHEA: *(Angered)* Gone.

LILLIE: *(Soberly)* I know, I should have known . . .

ALTHEA: And salvation is gone as well. There is a reason for us to be here, our parent's house, old and gone dry. The shadows of years pausing in a space. There is a reason. Sin and punishment predestined. *(Flatly)* The only thing you can anticipate is dying.

LILLIE: *(Rising)* I thought maybe . . .

ALTHEA: That you could anticipate joy?

LILLIE: *(Calmly)* A little joy.

ALTHEA: *(Sharply)* No. Only dying.

LILLIE: There are things worse than dying. Living can be worse than dying. Living with pain, living without joy, living without the expectation of . . .

ALTHEA: Anything except dying. That's all you can look forward to. *(Smugly)* I can look forward to the paper every day. I can know what's going on out there. Even with you dirtying the paper I still know. So . . . we take the days and weeks and times that run together and make a life.

LILLIE: *(Crossing to the chest upstage left)* Would you like the water now? The ice is gone.

ALTHEA: Bring it here. I'll try it.

LILLIE brings her the glass.

The glass is frosted, but it has run, the frosting. *(Tasting)* It'll do. I'll drink it. It's not right, but I'll drink it.

LILLIE: *(Earnestly)* Thank you.

ALTHEA: You're welcome. Ah, you see . . . there is politeness left in this house. Two well bred ladies, spinsters, living a life together. . . . We may not always say please, but we can say thank you.

LILLIE: And you're welcome.

ALTHEA: *(Lighter)* Mother would be proud to see her daughters. If Gen hadn't died what fun we might have had.

LILLIE: And William.

ALTHEA: *(Shaking her head)* William wouldn't have adjusted. It's as well. But Genivieve . . . which part would she have wanted?

LILLIE: She's been dead thirty years, and William forty. I can't know what they'd want today.

ALTHEA: Well, I can. People don't change as they grow older, they simply fix. The submissive stay submissive, and the strong grow stronger. It's just that simple. There is less complexity of character than people think.

LILLIE: They've been gone so long, I don't think I would know either of them if they walked into this room tonight. Do you? *(She walks down to the center chair.)*

ALTHEA: If they walked into this room tonight in the form in which they died or as they would be twenty, thirty years older? Which? *(Wheeling her chair to sit by LILLIE)*

LILLIE: I'm not sure I'd remember them either way.

ALTHEA: Of course I'm younger than you. My memory is better.

LILLIE: *(Defensive)* I remember many things.

ALTHEA: All inconsequential. As the time of age falls across our backs the one thing we cannot bear is change of role. That's because we've learned it well and long. The only truly unbearable factor . . . not dying, that's bearable . . . is to change position. *(Almost gently)* Don't you think?

LILLIE: *(Turning away)* I don't think I think anymore.

ALTHEA: *(Quickly back with her most unpleasant tone)* No, you don't. But then you never did.

LILLIE: *(Defensively)* But I taught school all those years.

ALTHEA: *(Lightly)* Whatever gave you the idea that teachers think? The only thinkers are creative people. Artists. . . Poets . . . *(Proudly)* Mostly poets. They never stop thinking.

LILLIE: *(Petulantly)* Teachers do think.

ALTHEA: They do not, they parrot. Polly, polly, pretty polly. *(A pointing gesture)* You've been a dun colored parrot for eighty years.

LILLIE: Stop . . .

ALTHEA: *(Superciliously)* With a mauve tail. *(Enjoying)* and eyes of no color, like a turtle. *(Regally)* Sister Lillie, flat and bent, head awobble without intent.

LILLIE: *(Loudly)* I can't bear your horrible poems.

ALTHEA: Nonsense, it's the fear of my kindness that terrifies you.

LILLIE: Stop.

She runs across the room right and puts her fingers to her ears. ALTHEA follows quickly. LILLIE walks as fast as she can to the left door.

I'll walk out of this room.

ALTHEA: *(Laughing)* No, you won't. *(Following)*

LILLIE: I will, I will, I will. *(her voice rising)*

ALTHEA: *(Laughing loudly)* You won't, you won't, you won't.

LILLIE: Stop it, Althea. I can't bear this game again.

ALTHEA: *(Prodding an old, old game)* You can, you can. Bear, bear. Sister Lillie . . .

LILLIE: *(With as much violence as she is capable of)* I said to stop it.

She crosses quickly to the day bed and sits, ALTHEA right behind her.

ALTHEA: Sister Lillie, was a teacher, mimicking another teacher, mimicking another teacher. Knowledge standing, couldn't reach it. *(Sweetly)* But ever, ever could she teach it.

LILLIE: *(Pleading)* I can't stand it tonight. Not tonight.

ALTHEA: Same as last night and tomorrow night.

LILLIE: Please, Althea, not tonight. Mrs. Grim . . . anticipation . . . please . . .

ALTHEA: Lillie, sister . . .

LILLIE: *(Her lips pursed)* I'm going to be angry.

ALTHEA: *(Playfully)* How frightened I am! Sister Lillie found her stage, played her role and not so badly. Until she tried to change the play. Sad, sadder, saddest, sadly. *(Shaking her head)* That wasn't very good. Requires refinement. What do you think, Lillie?

LILLIE: If insanity was possible for me. If I could go quickly, quietly mad . . .

ALTHEA: Pergande's don't go mad. They die, but never go mad.

LILLIE: Your poetry . . .

ALTHEA: Is not always perfect. I said the last was not so good. You heard me say. I am not the kind of artist who thinks everything I do is perfect. *(Pointedly)* Now listen quietly, I've been working on this all day.

LILLIE: I won't.

ALTHEA: You will, because you have no choice.

LILLIE: *(Quickly)* I do have a choice. We all have choices.

ALTHEA: *(Slowing a little)* No. There is a time in life when we lose that. And we both lost ours a long time ago.

LILLIE puts her hands to her ears again.

Take your hands down, I'd hate you to miss this. I've worked so hard. *(Firmly)* I said take your hands down.

LILLIE: *(Whimpering)* No . . . no . . .

ALTHEA: *(With some gentleness)* Yes. Take your hands from your ears. I do not wish to yell. I do not wish to stress my voice. When Sappho sings the world must listen. And you're the only audience. . . . *(Turning)* Very well, you cannot deafen yourself forever. And I have enormous patience. What an actress I would have been. If I had had the chance. *(Bitterly)* But I didn't. *(Wheeling back to LILLIE)* You are going to listen and you are going to listen now. *(Shouting)* Unplug your ears. You *will* hear me.

LILLIE: Not now, I can't now. Not tonight.

ALTHEA: *(Viciously)* I'm sick of you now. I have spent the better piece of the day thinking. I am never silent in my mind. I have worked and you will hear me. Because it is a masterpiece of poetry.

LILLIE begins to cry softly, she drops her hands from her ears.

Carefully listen, now.

LILLIE stares at her.

Let us make an illusion, you and I, that we have sometime loved each other, that we have felt . . . *(The doorbell rings)* . . . affection.

LILLIE: *(Rising)* The doorbell.

ALTHEA: *(Worried)* I heard it. I haven't heard the doorbell ring after dark in a decade. Must have some meaning.

LILLIE: *(Fearfully)* Must have some meaning. *(Looking about for a place to hide)*

ALTHEA: *(Quickly)* Meaning someone is at the door ringing.

LILLIE: No one ever rings our doorbell after dark.

ALTHEA: I know. . . . Answer it.

LILLIE: I'm afraid.

ALTHEA: *(A threat)* Answer it.

LILLIE: I'm afraid.

ALTHEA: Of what? What can be done that would impair us? Nothing. Of course you don't know it, but there is nothing in this world or any world for us to fear. Go to the door.

LILLIE takes a hesitant step toward the hall door.

Go on! Whoever it is may go away. *(Menacing)* I'd hate that.

LILLIE crosses to the hall door and exits.

I'd really hate that. *(Calling)* Don't stand at the door talking. If there is a caller bring them right in. If it is a mistake send them away. Do you hear me, Lillie?

She sits quietly thinking. There is a rumble of conversation in the hall.

Come in. Lillie, bring them in here.

LILLIE enters hesitantly with CLOVIS MITCHELL. He is twenty-six, dressed in poorly fitting clothes, and horribly deformed. He walks with great effort, his right leg being a good four inches shorter than his left and his right arm paralyzed. However, his face is beautiful as that of a slender Boticelli angel.

LILLIE: *(Simply)* This is my sister, Althea Pergande.

ALTHEA: *(A gesture of welcome)* Come in young man, come in.

He hands her a card.

Clovis Mitchell, assistant, Church of the Living God. . . . You're from the tent revival down the street.

CLOVIS: *(A smile angelic)* Yes.

ALTHEA: *(Searching his face)* I have been reading about you in the paper.

CLOVIS: *(Modestly)* We took a little ad.

ALTHEA: It was on the obituary page. I saw it right away. And a neighbor told my sister Lillie that you were there.

CLOVIS takes a step nearer.

CLOVIS: We've been there three nights, this is our fourth night.

ALTHEA: Interesting work, is it? Preaching and traveling.

CLOVIS: I don't preach.

ALTHEA: Oh?

CLOVIS: I am not gifted. I just try to lead people to our pastor. He is a great preacher. My job is to bring people to him. I witness, but I don't preach.

ALTHEA: *(Smiling)* Did you come to lead *us* to him?

CLOVIS: *(A step forward)* Yes. I want to lead everyone to him.

LILLIE: *(Crossing down)* A neighbor told me tonight, Mrs. Grim, down the street told me . . .

ALTHEA: Mrs. Grim told my sister that she had been and was young again.

LILLIE: *(Impulsively)* And she looked it. She smiled, as old as she is, she smiled.

CLOVIS: *(Humbly)* The preacher does things like that, he makes the old ones young again, he makes the young ones age in mind. . . . *(Almost a prayer)* He inspires us to find the best of our qualities and make more of them. Might I sit down, walking is not easy yet.

LILLIE: I'm sorry, of course. *(Leading him to the chair, center)*

ALTHEA: I can understand that. Take the chair. *(Indicating the chair center near the day bed.)* As you can see I don't walk. I haven't walked in the longest time. I had polio. Sister Lillie there brought it to me as a gift for my birthday. *(She wheels her chair closer to him.)* My infirmity is obvious to the world. So is yours. *We* have a handicap.

CLOVIS: *(Quick)* Or a blessing.

ALTHEA: I don't look on it as a blessing. Are you a polio case?

CLOVIS: *(Matter of factly)* I was born this way.

ALTHEA: *(Looking at LILLIE)* I wasn't. I walked and remembered walking. I ran. You don't remember walking, it's not so bad.

CLOVIS: I suppose not. I tire easily, I don't mind. Walking . . .

ALTHEA: *(Looking at his legs)* More like waddling. Ducklike.

LILLIE: *(Shocked)* Althea.

ALTHEA: Be still, Lillie. *(To CLOVIS)* My sister interferes occasionally. I . . . am a truth speaker. At my age there's no reason not to be.

CLOVIS: *(Laughing)* You're right. *(To LILLIE)* It's true, I do waddle like a duck. When I was a boy, the other fellows would follow me to school. . . . *(He makes a quacking noise.)* They still call me duck legs Mitchell at home.

LILLIE: Cruel. *(She looks at ALTHEA with meaning.)*

CLOVIS: *(Lightly)* I didn't mind.

ALTHEA: Of course not. He faces fact. Lillie, if you'd stop trying to hide your shaky old hands, you'd be better off.

Just hold them out and let them tremble in the wind. *(To CLOVIS)* Don't you think, young man?

CLOVIS: We each have a way of doing things, I don't know mine is better than anyone else's.

ALTHEA: *(Roughly)* You're too young to be sure of yourself.

CLOVIS: Not really . . .

ALTHEA: How old are you?

LILLIE: My sister doesn't mean to . . .

ALTHEA: *(Cozily)* I asked him how old he is.

LILLIE: Please, Althea.

CLOVIS: *(Lightly)* I'm twenty-six.

ALTHEA: You look older. I guess it's the pain.

CLOVIS: I have no pain.

ALTHEA: *(A point to make)* Then you . . . don't feel for other people?

CLOVIS: No. I can only feel myself. I try . . . I can try to understand how other people might feel. But I can't. *(He rises.)*

LILLIE: *(Crossing to him)* Don't get up.

ALTHEA: *(Her facade of bitterness completely gone)* No, stay a while and rest.

CLOVIS: *(Smiling)* I can't. I want to reach so many people. We had only twelve last night. In a tent that holds a thousand, there were twelve people. I had walked all day, I talked to hundreds. *(With great innocence)* Fifty people said they'd come, but only twelve came and some of those I didn't even see before. I don't have much time left. It'll be time to start soon.

LILLIE: *(Impulsively)* I want to come.

ALTHEA: *(To LILLIE)* Don't be ridiculous, your head jumping back and forth would disturb everyone there. You don't go out anymore. . . . *(To CLOVIS)* And of course, I don't go out anymore. *(Wheeling herself toward the window)* You see, I can't even get into the window. I don't see the sun. I don't see people. *(Turning around)* This is my universe. For sixty years almost.

LILLIE: *(Child-like)* I want to go.

ALTHEA: Nonsense. You'll stay here. *(To CLOVIS)* My sister is foolish enough to think she would be made young, the palsy gone, if she could get there. *(To LILLIE)* How would you get there, you don't know your way around the world anymore?

CLOVIS: *(Smiling)* I would take her.

ALTHEA: *(Laughing, her head thrown back)* The lame leading the lamer. *(Laughs)* What a pair you two would make. *(Wheels downstage center)*

LILLIE: *(Blurting)* My sister can be unkind.

CLOVIS: *(Crossing to the door)* I'll come back at a quarter of eight. I'll take you. *(Kindly, to ALTHEA)* You'll see, it'll be all right. *(Turning back)* Why can't *you* go? I'll push you.

ALTHEA: *(Moved)* No, I'm afraid I couldn't go . . .

LILLIE: *(Crossing to her and kneeling slightly)* Please, Althea, let's try. You say so often, what do we have to lose, whatever's waiting can happen now. Couldn't we try?

ALTHEA: No. There is no place for me out there. Or you either for that matter.

LILLIE: *(With more enthusiasm than she has felt in a long, long time)* Please, couldn't we . . .

ALTHEA: *(Undecided)* Give me a while to think it out. *(To CLOVIS)* How long will you be here?

CLOVIS: *(A step toward her)* Tonight's our last night. *(Apologetically)* I wish I could have found you before. *(With passion)* But it's not too late. It's not too late.

LILLIE: *(Pleading)* No, Althea. It's not too late.

ALTHEA: *(Sharply now)* I said I'd study it. I will. I didn't say no.

LILLIE: *(Disappointed)* But you will. You always say no.

ALTHEA: *(Sharp)* I do not. I do not always say no.

LILLIE: *(Defeated almost)* You will, I know you will.

CLOVIS: *(To LILLIE)* Give her a time to think. I'll be back. *(He starts to go.)*

ALTHEA: *(Suddenly)* Wait!

CLOVIS: *(Turning)* Yes?

ALTHEA: *(A pause)* Stay a moment.

CLOVIS: *(With hesitation)* I have so many people to see.

ALTHEA: *(Quickly with bitterness)* Then we're not important. *(She turns her back to him.)*

CLOVIS: *(Quietly)* Everyone's important.

ALTHEA: But we're not. *(Turning back to him)* But we don't feel we are. No, go on. Find your crowds. We've managed so long, a little longer won't bother. *(She means it now.)* It's really all right. *(She smiles.)*

CLOVIS: *(Hesitant)* I can stay a little while.

LILLIE: *(Quickly)* And have some coffee.

CLOVIS: *(Smiling at her)* I'd like some coffee. I don't want to . . .

LILLIE: It's easy. I'll hurry. *(She walks toward the dining room.)*

ALTHEA: Yes, hurry.

There is a gradual change in ALTHEA. There is less sureness of meanness.

Don't stand there shaking, hurry and fix the coffee.

LILLIE quickly exits to the kitchen.

You see my sister is a person of no direction. She has required guidance. She has been intelligent, but she has needed to be told when and where to move. *(Looking at her legs)* If I had not been crippled . . . I would be here in all probability anyway, caring for her. I think perhaps that's what I have resented most . . . the knowledge that if I could have spent my life walking straight as an arrow, nothing really would have been changed. Do you know what I mean?

CLOVIS: *(Trying to understand)* I don't know. I don't understand a lot.

ALTHEA: *(With sweetness)* It takes growing old.

CLOVIS: I don't know that I will understand then.

ALTHEA: *(Smiling)* You'll have to find it out for yourself. The right time. *(Seriously)* Tell me, do you believe in your preacher?

CLOVIS: *(Thinking)* I believe he speaks with the voice of God. *(He is sincere.)*

ALTHEA: But you said that you can only feel for yourself.

CLOVIS: That is true, but I can hear with understanding and take the faith the way I hear it. Do you have faith?

ALTHEA: *(Laughing scornfully)* The faith! I have faith in my ability to control my world . . . here. Perhaps that's why I don't go out.

CLOVIS: Let me tell you a story. My arm *(He takes his right arm and shakes it with his left hand.)* is heavy, sometimes more than others. Today it was very heavy. I have walked the streets for three days. I woke this morning. My arm was like a lead pipe. I said I can't go today. I can't go out and drag this arm with me. And as I said this to myself, I heard the voice of God, *(Striking a pose)* The cross was heavy on the Via Dolorosa. So I pulled on my clothes and I walked the streets.

ALTHEA: *(She does not mean to be unkind.)* How ostentatious of you to hear that.

CLOVIS: *(Crestfallen)* Yes, perhaps it was.

ALTHEA: A rationalization.

CLOVIS: Perhaps.

ALTHEA: *(Suddenly a thrust)* Why do you believe in him? The preacher.

CLOVIS: *(Simply)* Because he is kind.

ALTHEA: *(Unbelieving)* Because he is kind?

CLOVIS: Yes.

ALTHEA: Nothing else?

CLOVIS: When he leaves people they are kinder to each other. *(He is slightly defensive.)*

ALTHEA: *(Trying to nettle, to control)* There are kind people everywhere.

CLOVIS: I don't deny it.

ALTHEA: Then why him? You follow and drag your arm along. For what? I'll tell you what. Your own self-agrandizement. You want to see in eyes . . . what a wonderful man is . . . What's your name?

CLOVIS: Clovis . . . Clovis Mitchell. I hadn't thought about it like that. Perhaps I do. But if I can contribute even that way, does it matter so much? Does the motivation for goodness require goodness?

ALTHEA: *(Pushing)* For it to be real it does. Let me tell *you* a story. About me. I was going to be an actress. I memorized Roxanne, Celia, Juliet. I learned them all and I never got to use them. I was twisted in a wringing motion and left *(Simply)* like this. And all the words were wasted. Useless. *(Lightly)* So I became a poet, a poetess. And no one ever read any of my poems, because none of them were ever published. So I told them to my sister, who has such fierce needs. *(Turning from him slightly)* It is not enough to hold the poems in your head.

CLOVIS: *(Excitedly)* Exactly. It is not enough to touch kindness and not share it.

ALTHEA: *(Somewhat taken aback)* Something one creates is different from an ideal.

CLOVIS: This is no difference.

ALTHEA: I don't care for theology.

CLOVIS: *(Quietly)* I *care* for everything.

ALTHEA: Honestly?

CLOVIS: *(A moment's study)* I think so.

ALTHEA: *(Believing him)* Before my sister brings the coffee, I have not been kind to her . . . because she did not want kindness.

CLOVIS: *(Earnestly)* Everyone wants kindness.

ALTHEA: *(Shaking her head)* Not everyone. Some want to be controlled, to be kicked in one way or another. That's the way Lillie is.

CLOVIS: *(Very gently)* Is this your rationalization?

ALTHEA: *(A point against her . . . she accepts with a smile.)* We reverse our roles.

CLOVIS: *(Knowing he has gained a point)* Often.

ALTHEA: An exercise. Human contact is an exercise.

CLOVIS: *(Suddenly)* Please come tonight. I think you may learn something. Something of value.

ALTHEA: I don't know. I have too much to lose, too little to gain.

CLOVIS: *(Softly)* What do you have to lose?

ALTHEA: *(Simply)* You couldn't understand.

CLOVIS: I would try.

ALTHEA: *(Coming closer to him)* All right. Let me explain my sister. She has been a very passive gentle thing . . . all her life. As a child she cried when leaves fell from the trees, when flowers died.

CLOVIS: I can see her gentleness.

ALTHEA: And she could do nothing to prevent dying and aging. . . . *(Smiling in remembrance)* We had funerals for flowers. There is a cemetery for marigolds in the back yard.

CLOVIS does not comprehend.

You see you cannot understand. *(She turns from him somewhat.)* Because I still do not really understand either. Somehow she fixed on guilt and its expiation. *(Turning back to him)* There, I'm being much too serious.

CLOVIS: No . . . you have needed someone.

ALTHEA: Yes, someone to talk to. I forget my role. It is very difficult for me to be myself. *(Laughing softly)* I don't always remember who I am.

CLOVIS: *(Not understanding, he tries to turn the conversation)* You could sit on the front row.

ALTHEA: Your preacher could help me be myself?

CLOVIS: *(Eagerly)* Yes, he can do that too.

ALTHEA: With twelve out of fifty who came. You are a parable.

CLOVIS: No. I don't mean to be.

ALTHEA: Your preacher is not God?

CLOVIS: Oh no. He speaks well. He helps people to help each other. That's all. I never meant . . .

ALTHEA: *(Laughing)* It's all right. When you are young, you can be so very earnest. I tease. I've had to. *(Seriously)* You have brought something with you tonight. Do you know what it is?

CLOVIS: What?

ALTHEA: A faint, far, feel of hope. *(Pleased with herself)* That's an alliteration.

CLOVIS: *(Beginning to twist in his chair)* I don't know what that means.

ALTHEA: Nothing. Just a figure of speech. *(In a very cross voice)* Lillie, hurry up in the kitchen. I don't know why you take so long to do everything. *(Louder)* Don't forget about the newspaper. *(To CLOVIS)* The concept of kindness can be . . . the opposite. Don't you think?

CLOVIS: *(Losing interest)* I don't know. *(He is growing impatient to leave.)*

ALTHEA: *(Aware)* You wish to leave, don't you? There is such fatigability in doing good.

CLOVIS: *(Shaking his head)* No. I want people to hear him tonight. More than a dozen. There are other streets and almost no time at all.

ALTHEA: *(Calling)* Lillie!

LILLIE: *(Off-stage)* I am.

ALTHEA: *(To CLOVIS)* She'll be here in a minute. You will have your coffee and you shall go. On your way back, stop here and I'll let you know if we can go.

CLOVIS: You will be happy if you go. I promise that.

ALTHEA: *(Musing)* Can happiness happen so easily?

CLOVIS: It has, it has. I've seen it.

ALTHEA: Then I should like to see it. Young man, I am an old cynic, I am not unwise. You have no idea how much I have learned . . . *(A soft laugh)* from the obituary page.

LILLIE enters with a tray, three cups of coffee.

LILLIE: *(To CLOVIS)* I did not know how you liked it.

CLOVIS: Anyway . . . black.

LILLIE: I thought you might. *(To ALTHEA)* I tried to do yours just like you want it, if you want coffee.

ALTHEA: Indeed I do.

LILLIE gives them each a cup.

Smells very nice. *(She tastes it.)* Lillie it's wonderful. I never tasted coffee so good.

LILLIE: *(Incredulous, the first kind word from ALTHEA)* I. . . I. . . I. . .

CLOVIS: *(Quickly)* It is good. You make a fine cup of coffee, Miss Pergande. And I think your sister is planning to come and hear the pastor.

LILLIE: Oh, Althea, could we?

ALTHEA: Perhaps. I think we might. With the help of this young man I think we might.

LILLIE: *(Taking her cup to the window, she sits)* Do we have the right clothes?

CLOVIS: *(Turning to her)* It doesn't matter what you wear. You're both fine just as you are.

LILLIE: This? *(Indicating her dress, ashamed)*

CLOVIS: Is fine.

ALTHEA is thinking.

The Lord looks with favor on the meek and poor.

ALTHEA: *(A gentle warning)* That's ostentation.

CLOVIS: *(Turning to her)* I'm quoting. I do not speak for God.

LILLIE: When is the meeting?

CLOVIS: In about an hour. I'm trying to fill the first aisle anyway. It is the last night. Tomorrow we'll be somewhere else.

ALTHEA: Where?

CLOVIS: I don't know. It doesn't matter. *(Standing)* Thank you for the coffee. Miss Lillie, it was the very best coffee I ever had. Miss Althea, you make me think. I've got to rearrange my mind a little.

LILLIE: *(Rising)* Thank you for coming. We've held you long enough.

ALTHEA: *(Thoughtfully)* Yes, we have. Thank you for coming. *(Suddenly)* We *will* go. Lillie, what have we got to lose? We *will* go. With a little pride. Young man, is it all right to go with a little pride?

CLOVIS: I think in whatever guise you go you gain something. Well, you see for yourself. *(Crossing to the door)* I want to give you something . . . *(He puts his cup on the library table)* I want to say a prayer here with you.

ALTHEA: *(Quickly)* I thought you said you didn't preach.

CLOVIS: I don't. But I do pray.

ALTHEA: I don't think we're ready for prayers yet. Lillie, do you? What do you want?

LILLIE crosses to the door.

LILLIE: *(A new tone for her, a stronger voice)* No, not now. I . . . don't think we're ready for prayers.

CLOVIS: All right. Then I want to give you my book *(He takes a pocket book version of the New Testament from his pocket.)* It's all we can give. *(Sadly)* We don't have money. I'll be back in a little while. I'll be proud to take you . . . you'll be bright stars, the brightest there. *(A building exhultation)* And after the service, I'll bring you back here and Miss Lillie, you can fix more coffee and we can talk of dreams. We can talk of dreams.

He quickly exits into the hall. LILLIE follows, the door is heard closing and she rapidly reappears. LILLIE is flushed, a high state of excitement.

LILLIE: *(Breathlessly)* Are we really going, Althea?

ALTHEA: If you want to.

LILLIE: I want to go if you want to go. I never thought *you'd* want to go.

ALTHEA: *(Lightly)* I never thought I would dare. Our young man Clovis has touched a chord someplace. *(Jocular)* If nothing more than to see Mrs. Grim made young.

LILLIE: And us. Maybe we'll smile.

ALTHEA: *(Smiling)* I'm smiling now. See. *(She smiles up to LILLIE.)* And maybe in the Spring, we can hire a boy to take us to the park. We'll see leaves and blossoms . . . and . . . *(Trailing off)*

LILLIE: *(Flatly)* There'll be many people in the park.

ALTHEA: I think maybe we can look at them.

LILLIE: *(Frightened)* The children didn't worry me. Not very much. It was . . . the . . . parents.

ALTHEA: *(Crossing to the table and picking up the Bible)* It's a Bible. He left us his Bible.

LILLIE: *(Crossing to the window)* It's very dark outside.

ALTHEA: I know, it's night.

LILLIE: There are people in the dark as well as in the park.

ALTHEA: *(Brightly)* I want to see Mrs. Grim smile. You did and I want to.

LILLIE: *(Rationally)* Mrs. Grim smiled.

ALTHEA: That's why we're going.

LILLIE crosses to her.

LILLIE: *(Worried)* Was the coffee really all right?

ALTHEA: Yes, dear. It was fine.

LILLIE: You never said it was fine before. You said it wasn't fit to drink.

ALTHEA: I was wrong.

LILLIE: I made it the same way I always do. First I boiled the water and scalded the pot and the . . .

ALTHEA: It was wonderful. I was wrong before. Lillie, I think perhaps it's time for a change.

LILLIE: *(Unhearing)* Then I put the coffee in . . .

ALTHEA: It was very good.

LILLIE: And the eggshell. That's for clarification. You always wanted everything to be so clear. *(Coming close to her)*

ALTHEA: *(Trying to get this across)* I said I might have been wrong. The way I did things might have been wrong.

LILLIE: Oh no. You weren't wrong. I didn't try hard enough to please you. I've always felt so guilty.

ALTHEA: It is time for guilt to go. A new basis.

LILLIE: *(With clear understanding)* There isn't time. There never was.

ALTHEA: I gave up too easily. I was afraid to try . . . afraid of failure.

LILLIE: In the dark . . .

ALTHEA: *(Quick)* We may find light. It's worth a chance. Lillie, is it worth a chance? It's too late to have anything left to lose. Isn't it?

LILLIE: *(Fearful)* In the dark are people. Suppose we are attacked.

ALTHEA: People don't attack people.

LILLIE: They do. You said they do. We can't ever go outside

again because we'll be attacked, you said it. I remember you said it.

ALTHEA: I was wrong.

LILLIE: What's wrong and right? How can I tell what's wrong and right?

ALTHEA: *(Gently)* I'll always tell you. I'll tell you, Lillie. You don't have to worry about it.

LILLIE: *(Becoming more and more agitated and pacing about the room)* I don't want to go.

ALTHEA: Yes, Lillie, you wanted to go.

LILLIE: *(Childishly)* I don't now. I don't want to go now. I thought I did, but now I know I don't.

ALTHEA: *(Pleading)* Dearest, try, let's try.

LILLIE: No.

ALTHEA: *(With infinite patience)* Just once, let's try.

LILLIE: *(Near hysteria)* You can't abdicate the responsibility.

ALTHEA: *(Gently)* I'm not. Lillie, sit down . . . for a moment. Let me explain it to you.

LILLIE: I am not a child to be explained to.

ALTHEA: I know you're not a child.

LILLIE: Then why do you treat me like one?

ALTHEA: *(Without rancor)* Oh Lillie. I am treating you like my sister.

LILLIE: I was guilty. It was all my fault. All the sins, all the pains . . .

ALTHEA: *(Still very gentle)* They've been gone so long.

LILLIE: Not long enough. *(Looking about)* They're not gone. They're here. Here where I want them to be. Look around you.

ALTHEA: *(Tired)* I don't have to look.

LILLIE: *(Belligerently)* I'm not going. I don't care what you say. I'm not going.

ALTHEA: *(Soothing)* All right. We won't go. Not this time.

LILLIE: *(Even more fearful)* What do you mean, not this time?

ALTHEA: Just what I said. There may be another time. You may feel better another time.

LILLIE: I won't feel better if I have to think there is going to be a time. You don't understand at all.

ALTHEA: I understand too well. *(Wearily)* Isn't there any other way?

LILLIE: *(Quieter)* No. We were happy once.

ALTHEA: We were young once, too. *(Sadly)* I think we have both expected too much.

LILLIE: *(Coldly)* You would throw it out the door, all the balance.

ALTHEA: Lillie, I am tired and I am very old. And I would like to spend a peaceful day.

LILLIE: *(Shouting)* You don't care about me. You never cared about me. You used and used us all. The only thing you cared about was domination. DOMINATION.

ALTHEA: *(Thinking aloud)* He'll be back.

LILLIE: Who? Who?

ALTHEA: The young man. Clovis . . .

LILLIE: *(Taking the Bible from ALTHEA)*

She crosses to the door. The front door is heard opening and closing, the bolts being drawn.

Now.

ALTHEA is crying softly.

I threw the Bible in the mud. He can't help but step on it. And I bolted the door and he can't ever get back in here again. Not ever.

She crosses to the windows and pulls the drapes tightly without looking out.

And they can't see in. And I don't care about your paper. Do you hear? I don't care about your paper anymore.

She stands in the center of the window and taking the scissors from the chair, she begins to slash at her needlepoint.

ALTHEA: *(Still crying)* Stop it. Stop. *(Rapidly, her voice quavering)* Sister Lillie bent and shaking, head awobble, knees shaking, killed her sister and her brother, killed her father and her mother.

LILLIE dazed, puts down the shears.

Saying it was inadvertent. Saying that she didn't mean it.

LILLIE: *(Softly smiling)* I am going to cover my ears, Althea.

ALTHEA: *(Rough)* You wouldn't.

LILLIE: I will, I will.

ALTHEA: Saying it was accidental.

LILLIE covers her ears, her face transfigured.

That the poison and the pistol and the other means of murder.

LILLIE slowly crosses to the day bed and lies down, her hands still covering her ears.

We're acts of God, coincidental. *(Turning away)* Lillie never harmed a flower.

LILLIE: *(Far away)* I can't hear you.

ALTHEA: Let us make an illusion, you and I.

The doorbell rings.

That we have sometime loved each other.

She crosses to the bed and covers LILLIE with a quilt.

Because of gentleness.

The doorbell rings again.

Knowing too much and knowing too little. Sleep a while, you are right. It is too late to change anything.

ALTHEA wheels her chair center and sits, her face hardened.

CURTAIN

Lee Pennington

RAGWEED

Dramatist Personae

Hand
Foot
Ragweed

Setting

A graveyard with three tall stones side by side center stage, these stones much taller than the others. No figures are on stage when the play opens. Music (guitar only) of song "Ragweed" is softly playing in the background. It is night but there is moonlight, accented blue. Figures move onto stage one at a time and each stands behind one of the three tall stones: first Hand from stage left, then Foot from stage right, then Ragweed from stage center.

HAND: *(to others)* Good evening.

FOOT & RAGWEED: *(together)* Good evening.

HAND: It's a lovely night. No, that can't be right. How can the nights anymore be lovely?

FOOT: Somewhere, to someone, it is a lovely night.

RAGWEED: Perhaps.

HAND: The night is never lovely, not by itself, and yet, that's all there is.

RAGWEED: To us?

HAND: To everyone.

FOOT: The moon is lovely.

RAGWEED: To us?

HAND: To everyone?

FOOT: To someone.

HAND: Somewhere the night with the moon is lovely to someone.

RAGWEED: Perhaps.

FOOT: Well, anyway, the night is.

HAND: The night is what?

FOOT: It just is.

HAND: It can't be just is. It has to be something.

RAGWEED: Perhaps.

HAND: Where have you been, Foot?

FOOT: Walking. What about you, Hand?

HAND: Holding.

RAGWEED: What about me? *(They both look strangely at him but say nothing)* I say, what about me? *(They still only stare. Ragweed clears throat)*

HAND: Must be hayfever.

FOOT: Yes.

HAND: Oh, let's ask him anyway.

FOOT: All right.

HAND AND FOOT: *(together)* Where have you been, Ragweed?

RAGWEED: *(smiling)* Spreading. *(Hand and Foot shrug)*

HAND: *(looking around graveyard)* Do you think we should meet here every time?

FOOT: *(shaking head yes)* It's the only place we all know.

RAGWEED: I know all the places. *(Hand and Foot look angrily)*

HAND: Let's pretend we didn't hear that.

FOOT: Let's.

RAGWEED: *(head down)* I'm sorry. *(Hand and Foot shrug)*

FOOT: No need. We're all beyond all that now.

HAND: Besides, even if it's the only place, it's not a bad place.

RAGWEED: Let's talk about before.

HAND: All right. I'll start. *(looks up to night sky as if thinking, preparing an oration)* Those were the days. *(long pause)*

FOOT: You're taking too long.

HAND: Always in a hurry. You ready?

FOOT: No.

HAND: *(to Ragweed)* You ready?

RAGWEED: I'm always ready.

HAND: Give me time. I'm thinking.

FOOT: *(starts laughing)*

HAND: Now what?

FOOT: You said, "Give me time." *(more laughter)*

HAND: What's wrong with that?

FOOT: You've got eternity. Do you think you'll need anymore than that?

HAND: I forgot.

FOOT: No matter. There's plenty of time to remember.

RAGWEED: Yes, and to forget again.

HAND: *(in agreement, shaking head yes)* And to remember again.

FOOT: Over and over.

RAGWEED: I thought we were going to talk about before.

HAND: *(remembering)* Yes. Those were the days. Then I thought I could do it all.

FOOT: Then you didn't know it all.

HAND: But I thought. *(looks at hands held in air)* These were the answer, the only one. They could hold a hammer, a plow, guide songs from a guitar, carve faces from the silent stone.

RAGWEED: *(pointing to stones)* And names.

FOOT: Hold a knife.

HAND: It didn't matter and still I wonder. I am what these are.

FOOT: You are what they do.

RAGWEED: Touch. No more than a wet dishrag.

HAND: *(glaring)* My all. *(looking at hands now held down)* Build and shape, destiny controlled.

RAGWEED: You forget the night. Did you hold the night?

HAND: As surely as I held the wind.

RAGWEED: *(smiles)* The wind, my constant lover.

HAND: You are all lover.

RAGWEED: I'm all over. *(smiles)*

FOOT: Let Hand tell his story.

HAND: Yet, those were the days.

FOOT: The days of walking, running.

HAND: *(stares for being interrupted)* Perhaps I did hold the wind, the darkness, even the sounds curling through leaves, the blackness whispering from my fingers.

RAGWEED: You stripped the land, made the rocks bleed, gave living streams the drink of death and thirst for more.

HAND: *(not listening)* Whispering from my fingers. I shaped the earth, darling of my dreams.

RAGWEED: Even I, flying on wind, able to love even stone, choked where my roots went down.

HAND: *(realizing what Ragweed is saying)* And what difference is it?

FOOT: No place even for me, I who am all motion.

RAGWEED: *(Shrugs)* Are we to know who we are? Or what we do?

HAND: What difference?

FOOT: I am where I am.

HAND: You are where you go.

RAGWEED: Or stay.

HAND: If I break glass am I broken glass?

RAGWEED: If you break wind you are broken wind. *(Foot and Ragweed laugh)*

HAND: Be serious.

RAGWEED: Sorry.

HAND: Perhaps we should not talk of before?

FOOT: Since everything is now?

HAND: Yes.

RAGWEED: No, I like to hear of before, even now.

HAND: *(looking at hands)* Five fingers wide. Is that all? I always thought it more.

FOOT: Why so?

HAND: All they did. All the building, the holding, the touching.

FOOT: The tearing down, the killing.

HAND: Yes, I suppose I must admit that too. I wonder why I never want to admit that?

RAGWEED: The ripping apart the land.

HAND: That, too.

FOOT: So there's no place for me to be.

HAND: And even then does it matter? I build. I shape stones and great structures rise into the sky. I tear down, and kill and men die and the stones and men become dust for new stones and men sometime beyond.

FOOT: What are you saying?

HAND: I'm not sure.

RAGWEED: Say it again.

HAND: I can't remember.

RAGWEED: Talk about before.

FOOT: Will that get us closer to the answer?

HAND: Who knows? When we decided to come here, we only promised to search for the answer, not to find it.

RAGWEED: Shall I talk of before?

FOOT: Let Hand finish. There is time for all our turns.

HAND: Shall I begin in spring?

RAGWEED: You've already begun once.

HAND: When time is forever, one can begin as many times as he likes.

FOOT: But he can never end.

RAGWEED: Is that the answer?

HAND: No, a question.

RAGWEED: Before. I want to hear of before.

HAND: First, before I begin again, I want to say something else.

FOOT: Do we have a choice?

RAGWEED: Here we have all choices.

HAND: And no choices.

FOOT: Even if we can't decide, let's decide anyway. Say what you want.

HAND: Are you sure?

RAGWEED: Foot is never sure. Go ahead.

HAND: The tearing down. I've been thinking of the tearing down, and the killing. I don't think it matters. If I tear up the land, it is torn land. If the earth tears up the land, if mountains rise screaming in the dawn, if earthquakes shatter the silence, if wind, rain wash all away into the sea until the sea becomes land, it is torn land. If I kill, man dies. If I do not kill, man dies. Whatever, the land is torn. Whatever, man dies.

RAGWEED: Rationalization.

HAND: What?

RAGWEED: Rationalization. You merely rationalize.

HAND: I build.

FOOT: And tear down.

RAGWEED: And rationalize. You come from a nation of rationalization. And guilt. You feel guilty; so you must rationalize.

FOOT: Look. More come. *(looks at audience)*

HAND: It will be awhile before they can see us.

RAGWEED: Before. Begin again of before.

HAND: I cleared the land, moved back the tree line till there was no line, only land. *(holding out hands)* These broke the earth, even built the plow before breaking, and held seeds before planting. These held life becoming.

RAGWEED: I was there with none of that. I needed only wind.

HAND: Then these guided, held destiny.

RAGWEED: Rationalization.

FOOT: Now that you are all memory, how would you want to be remembered?

HAND: The builder.

FOOT: But you destroyed more than you built.

HAND: Very well then. Say that I touched, that I came and touched. Say that I found a wilderness and brought it tame till the sorrow grew like swelling pain and I seek the wilderness again.

FOOT: It is gone. There is no return.

RAGWEED: I was always wilderness, and you and you who now know, even now fear it so.

FOOT: Whose turn now?

RAGWEED: Since I was first, I will also be last. Go ahead, Foot.

FOOT: I've forgotten the question.

HAND: It's so easy to get lost. I can't remember, but I think it had something to do with worth.

FOOT: Before or now?

HAND: I'm not sure.

FOOT: I'll talk of before. Perhaps we'll think of the question.

HAND: Have I already talked of before?

RAGWEED: Yes, I think so. *(Hand moves a short distance from the others and sits down and begins thinking)*

FOOT: First I became uneasy with the land and I searched new land, walked new tracks my own deep down till they grew old and I grew tired and I again searched new land. I have always gone like smoke on the wind—to all corners, even where the angels stood, and beyond.

HAND: You always go.

FOOT: Always. I hear a door open in the wind, with hinges squeaking like dark clouds, and I must go through. Even now there is the door. Even now there is the road, and if no road, a path and if nothing, I begin—knowing others will follow. Did you say worth?

HAND: I can't remember. I think so.

FOOT: Perhaps that is the answer. Nothing is deeper than the shoe.

RAGWEED: Maybe the question.

FOOT: Tracks are immortal.

RAGWEED: You forget the rain. It washes them away.

FOOT: Then I will make new tracks.

RAGWEED: Now? Look where you go down. You leave no mark.

FOOT: *(turns to look back the way he entered)* You're right, but still I go. Even now, I can go if I choose.

RAGWEED: Talk of before.

FOOT: Before. I don't know where I began—only that I did. I never knew, nor now, where I was going. Even when I stood still, it was my choice. Likewise to go. At first there were no paths and I made them. Then roads. It didn't matter. I could choose to go, although often I did not know why I did. Once I walked on water.

HAND: Captured rain. The tracks were gone before you stood.

FOOT: Once I stood on the moon.

HAND: Reflected sun. Even then the tracks were done.

RAGWEED: This land *(pointing)*. Where did you go here?

FOOT: Everywhere. Once this was a new, strange land and my coming was a mystery. Then the tracks grew old. Some you destroyed *(pointing to Hand).* Some the rain washed away. Some I think I only dreamed I made. I came from darkness into the light. Now it is darkness again.

HAND: Now you are all dream.

FOOT: Yes, but wherever I can dream, I can go. I've still that choice.

HAND: But only I can build a dream.

FOOT: Or tear one down.

RAGWEED: Is there no more before for you except your going?

FOOT: Deciding to go.

RAGWEED: Is it my turn?

FOOT: I can't remember.

RAGWEED: Then it doesn't matter. It will be my turn. I will talk of before.

HAND: How can you, Ragweed? You are neither memory nor dream.

FOOT: And you have no choice.

HAND: And you cannot build.

FOOT: Nor tear down.

RAGWEED: True. You can touch and you and they remember your touch. And you can choose to go, and go. Your touch fades with memory, and your tracks die in dreams. I am always.

HAND: Yet, you are worthless.

RAGWEED: I do not have to decide. If there is wind, I go. If there is none, I fall there, death wrapped around my shell, but life bursts out and I grow and wait for new winds to blow. Even in death, I am alive.

HAND: The answer, my friend, is blowing on the wind.

FOOT: What?

HAND: I'm not sure. I think it's from memory.

FOOT: Tell me again. Perhaps it's from dream.

HAND: I can't remember.

RAGWEED: I have no need for dream nor memory. I need only my lover wind.

HAND: And if there is no wind?

RAGWEED: Then I have no need.

HAND: If you have no memory, how can you talk of before?

RAGWEED: I am always.

HAND: Is that enough?

RAGWEED: It is all.

HAND: Still, is that enough?

FOOT: Look. More come. Without sound, they slip from there to here.

HAND: Perhaps they will know the answer.

FOOT: Or the question.

RAGWEED: And there. The clouds announce the first sun.

HAND: And the night's end.

FOOT: Should we greet them?

HAND: They cannot see us yet.

FOOT: Then we must follow the night?

HAND: Always.

RAGWEED: The sun will find me, burst away the shell.

FOOT: Will we meet here again?

HAND: Yes. By chance or choice.

RAGWEED: One question. If the land could speak, which of us would it choose?

HAND: It chose all of us.

(They begin walking around as if futilely attempting to greet the new ones, then exit very slowly back stage. The song "Ragweed" begins almost immediately after last speech)

"Ragweed"

The sun shaves the frost
From the cold, cold ground.
The hair of the blue wind fall. (chorus and
Come this time another year around first stanza)
And I won't be here at all.

The size of the hand
Is five fingers wide,
The foot as deep as the shoe.
Stars burn on a cold winter night;
So tell me why don't you.

Chorus.

Ragweed grows in yonder field;
He grows so green and tall.
Spreads his seeds everywhere,
Anywhere they will fall.

Chorus.

(curtain)

ABOUT THE AUTHORS

More detailed information about these and other Kentucky writers can be found in John Wilson and Dorothy Townsend's *Kentucky in American Letters*, in three volumes, Sister Mary Carmel Browning's *Kentucky Authors*, and in *Contemporary Authors* published by Gale Research.

HARRIETTE SIMPSON ARNOW, novelist, poet, short story writer, historian, was born in Wayne County in 1909 and spent her childhood at Burnside. After attending Berea College and the University of Louisville, she remained in Kentucky until World War II when she and her husband, Harold, moved to Michigan. They now live in Ann Arbor. Her histories include *Seedtime on the Cumberland*, *Flowering of the Cumberland*, and *Old Burnside*. Her novels are *Mountain Path*, *Hunter's Horn*, *The Dollmaker*, *The Kentucky Trace*, and *The Weedkiller's Daughter*.

WENDELL BERRY, poet, novelist, essayist, was born at New Castle (Henry County) in 1934. He taught for a number of years at the University of Kentucky, and he now lives at Port Royal where he writes and farms. His novels are *Nathan Coulter*, *A Place on Earth*, and *The Memory of Old Jack*. *The Broken Ground*, *Farming: A Handbook*, and *The Country of Marriage* are among his poetry collections. Essays include *The Hidden Wound*, *The Unforseen Wilderness*, *A Continuous Harmony*, and *The Unsettling of America*.

BENJAMIN BRADFORD, playwright, was born at Alexandria, Louisiana in 1925. He now lives in Paducah (McCracken County) where he writes and practices medicine. His plays have won many awards and have been produced in foreign countries as well as in the United States. *Where Are You Going, Hollis Jay?* is produced approximately one to two hundred times each year. Other plays include *Geometric Progression*, *The Anthropologists*, *Charcoals and Pastels*, *Princess*, *The Goats*, and *Loving Kindness*.

JANICE HOLT GILES, novelist, was born in Altus, Arkansas in 1909, but she lived most of her life in Kentucky. After working as secretarial assistant to the dean of the Louisville Presbyterian Seminary from 1940 to 1949, she moved with her husband, Henry, to Spout Springs in Adair County. She died in Taylor County in 1979. *The Believers*, *The Enduring Hills*, *Miss Willie*, and *Run Me a River* are among her most popular novels. *Wellspring* is a collection of autobiographical essays and short stories.

CAROLINE GORDON, novelist, short story writer and critic, was born in Todd County in 1895. She has taught high school and has worked as a reporter and feature writer for various newspapers. In 1924, she married Allen Tate with whom she co-authored *The House of Fiction*, a book of criticism. In 1959, she was divorced from Mr. Tate. Two collections of her short stories are *The Forest of the South* and *Old Red and Other Stories*. Her novels include *Penhally*, *The Strange Children*, *The Malefactors*, and *The Glory of Hera*.

A.B. "BUD" GUTHRIE, JR., novelist and short story writer, was born at Bedford, Indiana in 1901. He grew up in Montana, then came to Fayette County where he worked for *The Lexington Leader* for twenty-one years. Mr. Guthrie also taught creative writing at the University of Kentucky. He now lives in Choteau, Montana. In 1950, he won the Pulitzer Prize for *The Way West*. This novel, as well as others, has been made into a movie. Other novels include *The Big Sky*, *These Thousand Hills*, and *The Last Valley*. *The Blue Hen's Chick* is his autobiography, and *The Big It* is a collection of short stories.

THOMAS MERTON, philosopher and poet, was born in France in 1915, and he died in Bangkok, Thailand in 1968. He entered the Trappist Monastery of Gethsemani at Bardstown (Nelson County) in 1941 and spent the rest of his life there. Collections of his essays include *Thoughts in Solitude*, *Seeds of Contemplation*, and *No Man Is an Island*. Books of poetry include *The Strange Islands*, *The Tears of the Blind Lion*, *A Man in the Divided Sea*, and *Selected Poems*. *A Thomas Merton Reader* includes both essays and poems.

JIM WAYNE MILLER, poet and essayist, was born in Leicester, North Carolina in 1936. He came to Kentucky in 1954 and has lived here since. Currently, he is teaching German at Western Kentucky State University at Bowling Green (Warren County). His books of poetry are *Copperhead Cane*, *Dialogue with a Dead Man*, and *The Mountains Have Come Closer*. *The More Things Change the More They Stay the Same* is a book of ballads, and *The Figure of Fulfillment* is a translation of the poems of Emil Lerperger of Austria.

MAUREEN MOREHEAD, poet, was born at St. Louis, Missouri in 1951. She moved to Kentucky twelve years ago and now lives with her husband, Robert, in Louisville (Jefferson County). Mrs. Morehead teaches English at Central High School, and she is a Ph.D. candidate in English at the University of Louisville. Her poems have appeared in *Kentucky Poetry Review*, *Adena*, *Wind*, and *Pegasus*—all Kentucky magazines. She has also been published in out-of-state journals such as *California Quarterly*, *Kansas Quarterly*, and *Black Warrior Review*, and she is included in *Intro 9 Anthology*. *Morning Has Big Hands* is an unpublished collection of poetry.

GURNEY NORMAN, novelist and short story writer, was born at Grundy, Virginia in 1937, but he grew up in Hazard (Perry County). After he majored in journalism at the University of Kentucky, he returned to Hazard to edit the *Hazard Herald*. In 1968, he moved to California to serve as associate editor of *The Whole Earth Catalog*. During the 70's, he alternated teaching at Foothill Community College in California and at the University of Kentucky. He is now teaching creative writing at the University of Kentucky. *Divine Rights Trip* is a novel; *Kinfolks* is a collection of short stories, and *Ancient Creek* is a recording of stories.

LEE PENNINGTON, poet, playwright, and short story writer, was born in Greenup County in 1939. He has taught at Newburgh Free Academy in New York and Southeast Community College in Cumberland. He is currently teaching at Jefferson Community College in Louisville. His poetry collections include *Wildflower*, *Spring of Violets*, *Songs of Bloody Harlan*, and *I Knew a Woman*. *The Porch*, *Appalachia*, *My Sorrow*, *Coalmine*, *Foxwind*, and *The Scotian Women* are among his plays.

ELIZABETH MADOX ROBERTS, poet, novelist, short story writer, was born at Perryville (Boyle County) in 1886. She died in Springfield in 1941. While her health permitted, she taught; then she traveled between Colorado, Chicago, Kentucky, and Florida. Among her books of poetry are *In the Great Steep's Garden* and *Under the Tree.* Her novels include *The Time of Man, My Heart and My Flesh, The Great Meadow,* and *A Buried Treasure. The Haunted Mirror* is a collection of short stories.

JAMES STILL, poet, novelist, short story writer, was born in 1906 in Alabama, but he moved to Hindman (Knott County) in 1932 where he still lives. Among the schools where he has taught are Hindman Settlement School and Morehead State University. *Hounds on the Mountain* is a book of poetry. *River of Earth* is a novel, and *Way Down Yonder on Troublesome Creek* is a collection of Appalachian riddles. *On Troublesome Creek* and *Pattern of a Man* are collections of short stories.

JANE STUART, poet, novelist, short story writer, was born at Ashland in 1943, but she grew up in W-Hollow in Greenup County. She majored in Latin at Western Reserve University, and she holds a Ph.D. degree in Italian literature from Indiana University. She now lives in Gainesville, Florida with her husband and two sons. *Eyes of the Mole* and *White Barn* are books of poetry. *Yellowhawk, Passerman's Hollow,* and *Land of the Fox* are novels. *Gideon's Children* is a collection of short stories.

JESSE STUART, poet, novelist, short story writer, lives in W-Hollow (Greenup County). He was born there in 1907. His farm is now The Jesse Stuart Nature Preserve open to Kentuckians and the people of the United States. In addition to writing and farming, Mr. Stuart has also taught and traveled extensively. His books have been translated into many foreign languages. Among his most popular novels are *Taps for Private Tussie, Foretaste of Glory, Trees of Heaven, Hie to the Hunters, Mr. Gallion's School,* and *Daughter of the Legend.* Included in his autobiographical books are *The Thread that Runs So True* and *The Year of My Rebirth.* His poetry collections include *Man With A Bull-Tongue Plow, Album of Destiny, Kentucky Is My Land, Hold April,* and *The Seasons of Jesse Stuart. Tales of the Plum Grove Hills, Dawn of Remembered Spring,* and *A Jesse Stuart Harvest* are collections of short stories.

HOLLIS SUMMERS, poet, novelist, short story writer, was born at Eminence (Henry County) in 1916. He taught in Kentucky for a number of years before going to Ohio University where he is now Distinguished Professor of English. His poetry collections include *Seven Occasions*, *The Peddler and Other Domestic Matters*, *Start From Home*, and *Occupant Please Forward*. His novels include *The Weather of February*, *The Day After Sunday*, and *The Garden*. *How They Chose the Dead* is a collection of short stories.

ALLEN TATE, poet, critic, historian, was born at Winchester (Clark County) in 1899, and he died in Nashville, Tennessee in 1979. He taught at a number of colleges and universities and he edited the *Sewanee Review* before he became one of its advisory editors. His poetry collections include *Mr. Pope and Other Poems*, *Selected Poems 1937*, *Poems: 1922-1947* and *Poems, 1960*. *On the Limits of Poetry* and *Reactionary Essays on Poetry and Ideas* are books of criticism. *The Fathers* is an historical novel.

ROBERT PENN WARREN, poet, novelist, historian, short story writer, was born at Guthrie (Todd County) in 1905. He received the Pulitzer Prize for his novel, *All the King's Men* in 1947. He also won the Pulitzer for two collections of poetry, *Promises: Poems 1954-1956* in 1958 and *Now and Then* in 1979. His poetry collections include *Or Else-Poems/Poems-1968-1974* and *Selected Poems 1923-1975*. *Night Rider*, *Band of Angels*, and *A Place To Come To* are among his novels. *Circus in the Attic* is a collection of short stories.

FURTHER READINGS

Allen, James Lane
Bride of the Mistletoe, novel
A Kentucky Cardinal, novelette
The Choir Invisible, novel
Flute and Violin, short stories

Auxier, Sylvia
No Stranger to Earth, poetry
The Green of a Hundred Springs, poetry
With Thorn and Stone, poetry

Baker, Prentice
Down Cellar, poetry

Bale, Joy
Never Less Than Love, poetry
The Storm's Eye, verse narrative

Bingham, Sallie
After Such Knowledge, novel
The Way It Is Now, short stories

Burman, Ben Lucien
Mississippi, novel
Steamboat Round the Bend, novel
Blow for a Landing, novel
Everywhere I Roam, novel

Caudill, Harry
Night Comes to the Cumberlands, history
Dark Hills to Westward, historical fiction
The Senator from Slaughter County, novel

Caudill, Rebecca
The Far-off Land, historical novel
A Pocketful of Crickets, children's fiction
Somebody go and Bang a Drum, children's fiction
Did You Carry the Flag Today, Charley?, children's fiction

Cawein, Madison
Undertones, poetry
Kentucky Poems
The Poems of Madison Cawein
The Shadow Garden and Other Plays

Chaffin, Lillie D.
John Henry McCoy, novel
A Stone for Sisyphus, poetry
Bear Weather, children's fiction
A World of Books, autobiography

Clark, Billy
Song of the River, novel
Riverboy, novel
Goodbye Kate, novel
The Illiterate Spider and Other Stories

Clark, Dorothy Park
Just for the Bride, novel
Roll, Jordon, Roll, novel

Clark McMeekin
Show Me a Land, novel
Reckon with the River, novel
The October Fox, novel
The Fairbrothers, novel

Cobb, Irvin S.
Cobb's Anatomy, humorous essays
Back Home, stories
The Escape of Mr. Trimm, short stories
Exit Laughing, autobiography

Cotter, Joseph S.
Links of Friendship, poetry
Caleb, the Degenerate, verse drama
A White Song and a Black One, poetry

Crabb, Alfred L.
Supper at the Maxwell House, novel
Home to the Hermitage, novel
Home to Kentucky, novel
Peace at Bowling Green, novel

Davenport, Guy
Da Vinci's Bicycle, short stories

Davenport, Gwen
A Stranger and Afraid, novel
Family Fortunes, novel
The Bachelor's Baby, novel
Belvedere, novel

English, Logan
No Land Where I Have Traveled, poetry

Ethridge, Willie Snow
Mingled Yarn, novel
Summer Thunder, novel
I'll Sing One Song, autobiography
Russian Duet, autobiography

Fox, John, Jr.
Hell-fer-Sartain and Other Stories
Christmas Eve on Lonesome and Other Stories
The Little Shepherd of Kingdom Come, novel
The Trail of the Lonesome Pine, novel

Giles, Henry
Harbin's Ridge, novel

Greene, Jonathan
Scaling the Walls, poetry
Once A Kingdom, poetry
Peripatetics, poetry
Glossary Of The Everyday, poetry

Hall, James Baker
Yates Paul, His Grand Flights, His Tootings, novel
Getting It On Up to the Brag, poetry

Hall, Wade
The High Limb, poetry

Hardwick, Elizabeth
The Ghostly Lover, novel
The Simple Truth, novel
Seduction and Betrayal, essays

Harney, John M.
Cristalina, a Fairy Tale, poetry
Echo and the Lover, poetry

Johnson, Annie Fellows
The Little Colonel Series, children's fiction
Travellers Five, short stories

Litsey, Edwin Carlile
The Love Story of Abner Stone, novel
Stones for Bread, novel
Spindrift, poetry

Madden, David
Cassandra Singing, novel
The Suicide's Wife, novel
The Shadow Knows, short stories
Bijou, novel

Markham, Lucia Clark
Sonnets to the Beloved
Sonnets of the Long Return

Mayhall, Jane
Cousin to Human, novel
Givers and Takers I, poetry
Givers and Takers II, poetry

McMeekin, Isabel McLennan
The Bronze Hunter, poetry
Journey Cake, children's fiction

Merrill, Boynton
A Bestiary, poetry

Morton, David
Nocturns and Autumnals, poetry
Poems: 1920-1945
Ships in Harbor, poetry

Noe, James T. Cotton
Tip Sams of Kentucky, poetry
Tip Sams Again, poetry
The Legend of the Silver Band, poetry

Norman, Marsha
Getting Out, play

O'Hara, Theodore
O'Hara and His Elegies

Rice, Alice Hegan
Mrs. Wiggs of the Cabbage Patch, novel
A Romance of Billy-Goat Hill, novel
Lovey Mary, novel
Miss Mink's Soldier and Other Stories

Rice, Cale Young
A Night in Avignon, play
Collected Plays
The Best Poetic Works of Cale Young Rice
Bridging the Years, autobiography

Sherburne, James
Hacey Miller, novel
The Way to Fort Pillow, novel
Stand Like Men, novel
Rivers Run Together, novel

Simones, Charles
Witch Cry, poetry

Steele, Frank
Walking to the Waterfall, poetry

Stewart, Albert
The Untoward Hills, poetry

Taylor, Richard
Bluegrass, poems
Girty, history and fiction

Thompson, Anne Armstrong
Message From Absalom, novel
The Romanov Ransom, novel

Tevis, Walter
The Hustler, novel
The Man Who Fell to Earth, novel
Mockingbird, novel